For KING

DAVID

Treasureface.

thank Goodness,

Zwakefield

73

*Stunt Water*
the Buddy Wakefield Reader
1991–2011

ℭ℥

Edited by
Jeremy Radin and Andie Flores

Front Cover Illustration by
AJ Frena

Write Bloody Publishing
*America's Independent Press*

Austin, TX

WRITEBLOODY.COM

Wakefield, Buddy.
1st edition.


Interior Layout by Madison Mae Parker
Cover Design by Ashley Siebels
Cover Illustration by AJ Frena
Back Cover and Author Poster by David Ayllon
Proofread by Madison Mae Parker
Edited by Jeremy Radin
Assistant Editors: Andie Flores and Madison Mae Parker
Buddy Wakefield Typeface Image by Stanley Chow
Some They Can't Contain Cover Art by Jeff Harmon
Live for a Living Cover Art by Chris A'Lurede
Gentlemen Practice Cover Art by Chris A'Lurede


Type set in Bergamo from www.theleagueofmoveabletype.com


Printed in Tennessee, USA


Write Bloody Publishing
Austin, TX
Support Independent Presses
writebloody.com


To contact the author, send an email to writebloody@gmail.com

MADE IN THE USA

*STUNT WATER*

There was a typewriter
buried alive in that horse,
the one I rode to get out of the flood.

Buddy Wakefield

# STUNT WATER

# GENTLEMAN PRACTICE

*Editor's note: While the poems from each of Buddy's books are not presented in chronological order, the books from which they originally appeared are.

# FOREWORD

Created from his first three books of poetry, which are now out of print, *Stunt Water* offers classrooms and spoken word enthusiasts a comprehensive look at the pivotal works of Buddy Wakefield.

Skillfully edited by Jeremy Radin and Andie Flores, *Stunt Water* wastes no time staging an insightful, dynamic reading experience through the driven song lyrics and poems of Buddy's late teens/ early twenties (when this closeted gay college kid, who had been riding bulls for Jesus, first threw his redemptive musings into the mix by starting an open mic night in a Huntsville, TX, coffeehouse), to the gripping and pioneering works that would eventually rocket his spoken word career beyond the bars of Seattle (where his first appearances included a vegan café called The Globe, Seattle Poetry Slam at OK Hotel, and opening for an all-female punk band named Pink Chihuahuas) into the forefront of the performance poetry world.

Buddy Wakefield's story is huge. All of it. For the first time, we get a detailed glimpse at his starting point in the largely fearless, previously unpublished poem, "Disclaimer." From there, his work spreads out 360 degrees across ten years of touring. Starting with the days Buddy lived in his car earning keep as a touring poet, clear through to being backed by Norman Lear for the first ever Individual World Poetry Slam in 2004, until now; Buddy's poems are *still* being used to win collegiate forensics competitions; he's *still* opening for rock stars; and he's *still* being stylistically mimicked by poets and performers internationally. There is far too much to detail about Wakefield, his career and his accomplishments, so let me just say this:

1

If you've never been rocked back by the presence of purpose, this book is too soon for you. Tender, jarring and deeply human, *Stunt Water* is pulsing with the same electricity and honesty found in his live performances. Through all 145 pages of this roller coaster that I would stand in line to ride twice, I was goose bumped to the bone, racing towards the deep end, sucker punched and silenced. You will not find another writer more disarming in his humility, more brave in his hopes, or more brilliant in his lack of etiquette.

This book breaks laws, is dirty and riddled with rogues, but remains refreshingly void of shock value and gives the slip to tragedy. These raw, energetic, inadvertently consoling poems are clear writing on the wall for anyone approaching life after survival, a helpful map when navigating the unforgiving turns a path can take. As Brown University student, Emma Galvin, simply put it, "Wakefield is gentle and forgiving of the people and parts of this world that really need it, while compelling those of us who the world has treated so kindly to feel uncomfortable. I enormously respect that subversive element in his work and person."

*New York Times* best-selling author Cristin O'Keefe Aptowicz wrote, "Wakefield has had a profound impact on the contemporary Poetry Slam movement, both in his performance and writing style as well as how he has conducted his career." In her book, *Words in Your Face: A Guided Tour Through Twenty Years of the New York City Poetry Slam*, Aptowicz named Wakefield as "the modern poetry slam role model." She went on to say, "[Wakefield] sold everything he owned and toured the country, living out of his car when he wasn't crashing on couches. He was not the first slam poet to do this and certainly not the last, but he was definitely the most high-profile, and he really set the stage for what I like to call the 'Troubadour Movement' in slam, the whole desire simply to tour, to reach out and be with your community."

*Stunt Water* is rich with recovery, revisions and the restorative ink our mad world needs. I am much *much* better for having been here. In your hands is a ripcord. Don't be afraid to use it.

— *Andrea Gibson*

# SOME THEY CAN'T CONTAIN

[BUDDY WAKEFIELD]

# WORKS FROM
## *SOME THEY CAN'T CONTAIN*
### 1991–2004

*For the nomad, the nervous, the hunter, the zoo and for the catalyst of the instrument I played to get to you. For a bastard, his father, the perpetual lull and to the critic racing here for the words to write me off if I say it's for the grinning, the bearing and for the sprawled out into rage, and for their desperate amendments to keep my heroes out of range. It's for the eggshells you're walkin' on and to the circling ya do, and to the slow-approach-me-anything-goes, gear up to be reused in a poem for the marching, the watching, debating the dream, buttered-up and thirsty, imploding from the steam.*

# CONVENIENCE STORES

We both know the smell of a convenience store at 4 am
like the backs of a lot of hands.  She sells me trucker crack
(Mini Thins; legal speed). She doesn't make me feel
awkward about it. She can tell it's been a long drive.
It's only gonna get longer. She offers me
a free cup of coffee but I never touch the stuff.
Besides, I'm gonna need more speed than that.

We notice each other's smiles immediately.
It's our favorite thing for people to notice
our smiles. It's all either one of us has to offer.
You can see it in the way our cheeks stretch out like arms
wanting nothing more than to say

> *You are welcome here.*

She shows brittle nicotine teeth with spaces between each one.
Her fingers are bony, there are no rings on them
and she would love to get her nails done someday.
One time she had her hair fixed.
They took out the grease, made it real big on top
and feathered it. She likes it like that.

She will never be fully informed on some things
just like I will never understand who really buys Moon Pies
or those rolling wrinkled dried-up sausages
but then again, she's been here a lot longer than me.
She's seen everything
from men who grow dreadlocks out of their top lips
to children who look like cigarettes.

I give her my money, I wait for my change,
but I feel like there's something more happening here.
I feel like a warm mop bucket and dingy tiles
that will never come clean.
I feel like these freezers cannot be re-stocked often enough.
I feel like trash cans of candy wrappers
with soda pop dripping down the wrong side of the plastic.
I feel like everything just got computerized.
I feel like she was raised to say a lot of stupid things

about a color and I feel like if I were to identify myself
as gay, this conversation would stop.

It's what I do.
I feel.
I get scared sometimes.
And I drive.

But in one minute and forty-eight seconds I'm gonna walk outta here
with a full tank of gas, a bottle of Mini-Thins and a pint of milk
while there is a woman still trapped behind a Formica counter
somewhere in North Dakota who says she wants nothing more
than to hear my whole story (all ninety-two thousand seven hundred
and seventy-five miles of it).

I can feel it though, y'all: she's heard more opinions and trucker
small talk than Santa Claus has made kids happy, so I only find
the nerve to tell her the good parts, that she's the kindest thing
to happen since Burlington, VT, and I wanna leave it at that
because men – who are not smart – have taken it further,
have cradled her up like a nutcracker and made her feel as warm
as a high school education on the dusty back road
or a beer in a coozy.

I feel like she's been waiting here a long time for the one
who'll come two-steppin' through that door on eighteen wheels
without making her feel like it's her job to sweep up
the nutshells alone when she's done been cracked again,
who won't tempt her to suck the wedding ring off his dick,
but will show her, simply, love.

She doesn't need me or any other man but
she doesn't know that either
and I'm just hoping like crazy she doesn't think I'm *the one*
because the only time I'll ever see North Dakota again
is in a Van Morrison song late *late* at night, I promise.

I feel like she's 37 years old wearing 51 badly, dying inside,
like certain kinds of dances around fires, to speak through you,
a forest, if you weren't so taken with *sparks*.
But she was never given those words.
She has not been told she can definitely change

8

the world. She knows some folks do but not in convenience stores
and *not* with lottery tickets, so I finally ask her what I've been
feeling the entire time I've been standing there, still, gettin' scared
like I do sometimes, really ready to drive, I ask

*Is this it for you?*
*Is this all you'll ever do?*

Her smile collapsed.

That tightly strapped-in pasty skin
went loose.
Her heart fell crooked.
She said, not knowing my real name,

*I can tell, buddy, by the Mini Thins and the way you drive,*
*that we're both taken with novelty. We've both believed*
*in mean gods. We both spend our money on things that break*
*too easily, like people. And I can tell you think you've had it*
*rough, so especially you should know*
*it's what I do.*
         *I dream.*
*I get high sometimes.*
*And I'm gonna roll outta here one day.*
*I just might not get to drive.*

# A WASTE

We'll call her *Sweet Angel*: hugs herself
when she's stupid,
gets facials from a wonderful woman in the city
who talks like a landslide,
boys used to call her *Peach*.
The way she said it burned me up like a blown out tanning booth.
In an attempt to make me feel handsome
Sweet Angel said,

*If I was a girl your age*
*and I found out you were gay*
*I'd just think, ya know,*
                            *what a waste.*

Okay, hey, perky cheeks. If that was supposed to be
a compliment, please
don't ever send me a care package.

                    A Waste
            is more like when I stole a woman's trust, love
and virginity then broke her heart just to prove
to the fellas that I really like sex with women.

                    A Waste
            were all the ceiling lights I broke juggling
cheek bones and steel, gay and Texas, glass
ornaments made of closets that can easily hang,
hide, and stretch my dirty laundry on clotheslines
from San Mateo to Niagara Falls back to Texas
and you'll never see a thing.

Fourteen and fading. Parents on marriage
number eight. Me keeping all of it
                    hidden
up in the air like ducks in a row, ready
to go down during hunting season.

To some children, self-preservation and mirrors
will always look like a grown man with raw lips
and lockjaw whose heart pounds out so fast for safety
it sounds like ice picks
                              chipping holes
through the chest of a sculpture his parents
would have otherwise loved to show their friends.


            A Waste
                were the years without light
or smiles or worth spent in places it's not fair
for me to tell you about. Like the backs of adult
arcades where I learned that the only certainty
some human beings will ever know
is this:


              There's a naked man


                        and there's a dark
                                    room


                                          everywhere.


These are children who will not be told there is nothing
wrong with being human, who are not allowed to love
themselves despite their crimes, who will have no one
there to help them arrange chaos into alphabetical order
once they realize that sometimes being born is really
                                        inappropriate.


They will be haunted by their ability to hate you,
to give you back what they got from you. It's the quickest
slow death you'll never see          until the wind blows
          on a quiet day
and you ain't got nobody to hold. It is


            A Waste
like the hundreds of gallons of gas I burned
pulling off                          into the alley
so I could die
or scream
or clutch.

There will never be enough
back road in this world
to make you understand
how much I loved him.

A Waste
is a nine-year-old boy playing catch
with the roof of his garage
who already understands that his existence
makes for the perfect insult.

Gay.
*You're so gay*

a.k.a. *stupid* a.k.a. *dumb* a.k.a. *wrong mutherfucker*
*wrong wrong mutherfucker.*

Do have any idea how gross it feels
to have to hide inside the pile of lies it takes
to make you, Sweet Angel, comfortable?

Knowing me, it's easy.
You can still twist your hair and feel silly,
look up the word *tacky* and have a salad.
But when we're together you pull bread apart
with your fingers into bites sometimes so small
I gotta remind you, Peach,
It is okay
to be hungry.

12

# FRAN VARIAN'S GRANDMOTHER

> "It's been a long time since anyone's called her beautiful.
> It's been even longer since she heard she was bright."
> — Steven Arrowood


Fran Varian's grandmother told us
she caught a letter from Heaven
saying that the children of her children's generation
would be devils walking the earth.

When I hear this it somehow feels right.

It feels familiar, like the ghost story about the young couple
who break down near a town where a lunatic is on the loose.
Boy runs for help, remember? Girl hides. Covers up
in the floorboard. An hour later there is a single knock
on the car top, then another, steady, all night long.
When day breaks girl finds boy hanging upside-down
where the wind blows, knockin' his knuckles on the window
and on every dream I had the night I heard that hell.

Her words barge in and out of me now
but I don't know if that's twice a day or once a week
because each time still feels like the first.

*Devils,* she called us, *walking the earth.*

When I hear this, I can't move and I can't breathe.
Feels so much like ghost stories and bad dreams.
Makes me desperate to hold the hand
of Fran Varian's grandmother, not too hard, not as tight
as I'd like to. I'd keep it calm so I don't seem desperate
but I do. I get so desperate
to know if she caught a second letter saying anything
from anywhere up above that coulda mighta maybe mentioned
others, not devils, but others
with halos shaped like roller coasters
you'd stand in line to ride twice.

Others, who don't know how to tell you
and still remain humble
that it's been a long time
since anyone's called them beautiful
and it's been even longer
since they heard they were bright.

But Franny's grandma doesn't remember
catching any other letters. Just the one saying
that the children of her children's generation
would be devils walking the earth.

When I hear this, Mom, it hurts, hard, from my chest
like the dream with the fear of the man forever.
His fatness, all hate. He straddles like whiskers
my stomach and grins through my face.
The weight of his head, so blood red raked-up crusted
and thick. Spit. Eyes full out like a choke hold.
Teeth split. Ears twisted. Balled-off deaf now boy
goddamn would you keep it still.

And I do.

I get scared so still it feels like statues and wind
left in a garden behind some old white house
in a dead wheat field where if anyone would just yell *mercy*
maybe these lungs could finally fill but Fran Varian's grandmother
caught a letter from Heaven saying that the children
of her children's generation would be devils
walking the earth, so I gasp and pull
for a full breath of air
like air
is the only way out

# Now

wanna be a monk
wanna be hooked on junk
that makes me
feel for you

wanna live in a stained glass shack
wanna walk with a cross on my back
if that'll get me
closer to you

wanna be pure in heart
tear their talkin' apart
and be quiet now
just for you

wanna be the meek
wanna walk my calloused feet
on the softest grass
you ever grew

wanna be of every faith
wanna benefit from every grace
then give it all
back to you

gonna live now
turn these words around
and be entirely
new

# PRETEND

Pretend
on this side
there's an albino monkey
making bass in a jug with his tongue.

Pretend
on this side
there's a pitch black
woman dressed in a slow
tornado who looks so much like
the night time she turns almost blue
in the sun. She's gonna carry us through
this tune with Huntsville, Texas and The Soul-
Lifters Gospel Choir. That's my back-up diva.

Pretend behind me
it's just one
big
bang.

Now it's you.
Pretend you're just being yourselves.
Pretend you live for a living.
Pretend – inside your skin – you've got a friend
who's willing to give you everything you ever wanted
in exchange for all you've ever been.
Pretend you're more obsessed with this moment
and a little bit less with the way it ends.
And for a moment
pretend

in front of me
is a plywood lemonade stand
with a sign on the front that reads
*I've got no more lemons*
*just my OPINIONS*
*Yours*
*for A DIME-A-DOZEN today*
*and they're always gonna be on the table*
*but only some are gonna set you free.*

Okay now here's where I need you to believe
please. Believe that here stands a man
who pretends not to fall apart,
who gets so nervous his lips peel back
when we give any slack to the dark side,
who gets so god-solid scared
*yergonnawannatalkabouttomorrowagain*
that he'll pretend to stand and listen
with a sharp look on his face

while a monkey plays bass
bass

                        with a back-up diva
                     pullin' back-up faith

for this one-man cross-universe
relay race
to try and be more than human
beginning and ending
moment by moment
rolled over re-birthing again

because history is repeating itself in record time, y'all,
and we have got to stop acting like nothing's happening
when we've got six-billion dawning truths
setting six-billion different suns on you
but we six-billion gods are all still up in arms
over what it will cost to follow through
so that you can be me forever my friend
at the same time I get to be you

so you can rock me brother rock

                  and you can soothe me sister soothe

like one

big

bang

because I don't believe the big bang really happened yet.
I think a small bang mighta went *pffft*.

But the big bang
is just on its mark
set
and is really ready to go
kinda like a slow tornado
growing larger
than six-billion words
moving faster than a sky
flying farther away
from every square inch
of us racing birds.
It looks a lot like it would
if just one brain
in the heart of this place
rose up
to the actual size
of the actual voice
it actually contained
into just one head
singing just one song
with a word
and six-billion looks
on its face
to see a monkey play bass
to feel a back-up diva
with her back-up faith
goin' off,
like one
big

bang.

# Dear Angry Older People,

Next time you're wondering what's wrong with kids today,
you might wanna check out the examples you've been giving
us to work with.

If you ever wanna make sense *of* us you have to make sense *to* us
without telling us you're too old to walk that far.

You gotta try understanding *why* we like looking like rag dolls,
*why* we like looking like the way we feel and *why* we keep our senses
floored when it's you behind the wheel.

And if you ever really do wanna understand why we seem so angry,
well, for one: you told us we could be anything we wanted to be but
right now we're a little busy dodging bombs.

Okay, and two: rather than celebrating the gifts you've got we more
often see you blowing fuses over simple mistakes on dinner receipts as
if the waitress was purposely ramming you in the ass with dynamite
sticks and branding *kick me* signs on your faces.

It was an accident. You've got to calm down. Rethink this approach.
Ask yourself, "*Whaaaaat...* would Bill Murray do in this situation?"

I've seen fish hooked that keep more patience in their worst gill than
some of you have in your best mood. If you were a sandwich at a fast
food fiesta they'd call you the *McGrump*. You've got to get a grip.
Please. It's been another long day playing games in the schoolyard
trying to make sense for old people who won't be satisfied.

So I suggest you hush up, turn around and march those cranky butts
straight back to your rooms while me and your sons and daughters try
figuring out how to actually use all this forgiveness we found piling
up in the laundry you still haven't washed because you've been too
busy out prescribing all that hell and giving it away in hand baskets to
those who *SEND CASH! ACT FAST! CALL NOW!*

Well, this is me without my Prozac!

And this is me just shy of nicotine!

And *mutherfuckers* it's my second time to fail an anger management class so for the love of greatness please stop moving the hands of *my* clock to the time *you* had it made. I'm way too busy working out the kinks here. You didn't exactly wind this thing back up when you were through hosing down all the big bright violent warning signs we done lit up out in gangland and on down the road to Columbine where all these kids you can't seem to make any sense of would stop holding you so far off the edge of your seats if you'd start holding *yourselves* to the promises you make.

We know you're not perfect, because we're not.

And I know I'm not perfect.

But I believe I was meant to be.

# Disclaimer

In the decathlon of dysfunction I'm willing to bet my mother and
father's combined eight wedding rings that I'm bringing home
the gold

unless my Aunt Ruby steals it first and hocks it for pharmaceuticals
and vibrators that my Uncle Ron will never find out about because
he's too busy feeling up his own children

but don't get that pedophile confused with my first stepdad who was
pulling me raw in the bathtub by the time I was nine to make me his,
and changed my real name,

which deeply disturbed my real father even though he swore it didn't
right up until the day he pulled down the garage door, turned the
ignition, inhaled and choked

on his compulsive lies, his fake college ring, his fake bachelor's, his
fake masters, his fake PhD and his policeman's badge.

Yeah, I'd like to be normal, ya dick, but who are we trying to kid?
I've got a full disclaimer. It says *usually I'm everything, just not today.*
So next time

you need to read the goddamn disclaimer before you go sticking your
wires up in my brain and digging ditches in circles through the best
of my name and, frankly, rubbing me the wrong way because I never
rubbed up on you.

I'm also willing to bet two-thirds of the beatings I watched my
mother take, a month's supply of food stamps and the feeling of
justification I have for being disgusted by a system that throws around
the word *justice*

just as carelessly as it does the innocence of our children that I get
what it means to be a minority. I am the minority; one in six billion
who's taken it up the ass figuratively, literally, painfully, shamefully
and simultaneously.

21

We're talkin' a shame and a pain like napalm, back when guilt was riding shotgun on the tip of a cracked whip from my gut to my teeth, through my veins, up my nose, up my nose, up my nose and into my lungs. Both of them.

I can hallucinate on guilt alone. I learned to do that right around the time my psychic schizophrenic grandmother tried stabbing me to death because she was convinced I was giving her shock treatments

like they used to do back in the ward. That's the same grandmother who killed my 12-year-old cat while I was at school and said *they* did it. But she wasn't all bad. She at least had the decency

to let my four-year-old cousin live with her after *she* was forced to eat her own shit because *her* stepmom didn't like it that she had accidents.

So next time, before you go rain dancing around my fire trying to put me out because maybe I'm *not* normal like your yummy American pie, or maybe I am too intense and I don't remember how to forget about it when

everybody I know is giving head to stacks of money and canning all the juices from all the sex with all their lovers and saving it up for later in case the desperation gets so goddamn deep

they gotta go and fuck their own minds just one more time instead of throwing it all out and learning from this whole overexposed over-stimulated mess. Next time

read my fucking disclaimer, y'all: *I'm everything, just not today.*

Today I make a move on nothing
until it lifts me by the eyes
because if I don't come back to life this time
then it just wasn't worth the fight that I put up to stay alive.

And if this is too much for you... Oh,
I'm sorry.
Usually I'm everything,
just not today.

22

# CANNONBALL MAN

On the edge of my seat
at the end of my rope
where riddles bloom
where answers fold
I've got a 20-year story
still to be told
about a cannonball man
in the circus sideshow.

Now that mutherfucker
was ready to explode.
He had pressure pouring in
from every hole. They lit
his fuse. They watched him
blow and where he's gonna
stop, nobody knows

because they shot him off
over the cities and the plains
like lilacs across the sky
like a dove inside the flames
on a candle wax train to paradise

but distance began to spread
between the flight of his feet
and the weight of his head
and as he curled it all up
between his knees he caught
wads of sun breaking
up in the weeds

goddamn that cannonball man
unwound because to rise then fall
feels so profound when 2000 clowns
wanna pile from a car with a stretcher
full of mismatched cannonball parts

but no he picked up his brains
his eyes, his teeth, he gathered
his words and he made it all speak
then he backed off the show
with a well-lit fuse, stuffed himself
down in a cannonball tube

and with a free man's grin
he took to flight right past
the battling birds in the night
who had cannonball eyes
and cannonball teeth
cannonball balls
and cannonball wings

and with cannonballs stuck
between their beaks
they all shot down and
they broke on the streets

and as I looked up

with feathers in my eyes

on the edge of my seat
at the end of the line
I saw lilacs hummin'
across the sky
and a cannonball
inside the flames

on a candle wax train
to paradise.

# SOME THEY CAN'T CONTAIN

because I drop my jaw at fire when it's flying out my eyes
and I plunge my coiling wires in the water till I rise
above frogs and pop rocks
and boxes of roof tops
and the noises I can't outrun
even when I'm running twice the speed of sound already
and three times the speed of my blood

'cause everybody's got voices

and everybody's got some they can't contain

like my need to be redeemed
at any time, in any place
where I see my Jonathan Seagull
being tattooed on the fists
of men who fear we'll think what we think
about the laws they can't resist

so you can bring on your boogeyman
loading his fuss and gunning his fattening desire
'cause I've got bees on flowers
with honey on hold
for those made of gold but wrapped in wires
who keep themselves inspired
by the way they feel their spines
screaming sparkling gods
who gotta live by the way they shine

and this is not a dot-to-dot plot
or a battle on your god
of the makers of money
odd mockers of drum
who all peel and staple great gobs of Marge Maple
the girl they just gotta slum, no

this is my time and place

this is me saving my saved face

so if my heart starts to radiate
bold broken glass, man relax
it always pumps this fast
because I drop my jaw at fire when it's flying out my eyes
and I plunge my coiling wires in the water 'til I rise.

# MARBLES IN THE TREES

Y'all come around. Come on now. Pay no mind to the fumes.
I got somethin' to say about the folks doin' time in this room.
Y'all the walls' been whistlin' downright fattenin' yella-bellied tunes.
Check the mirrors for yer orders.  Grab a seat in the blues.
Yer waitress be with ya soon as she tends to her perfume.
     *Annie!*

Now that's one chicken, no head. One backbone, loose.
One muscle-bound contraption with a fool's gold tooth.
But the broiler's frozen down so yer gonna hafta take it raw
and excuse the dishes, they wouldn't fit in our sink
full of dirty thoughts.

Hey Dingy Grin, how you been? I see there's thoughts in yer lap
and yer killin' that tobacco while it's killin' you back.
Nah, now it's good to know yer totin' those excuses in yer sack
'cause yer gonna need'm if we bring back yer past.

And *you*, what's yer name? Why the wait?  Make a choice.
We can serve it on the rocks or we can spike it with a voice.
But if you ain't hungry or thirsty then you gotta stop makin' noise
'cause I best be fixin' orders for the starvinest girls and boys.

Ahh y'all, we could be outside playin' marbles in the trees
watchin' a spotless future move us jigglin' fireflies in the breeze.
But no, here we go again mouth agape a-waitin' for someone free
to feed us what we want when what we got is all we need.

We ain't all that hungry, just a dash misled.
How 'bout I have that waitress bring some
somethin' to keep yer heads?
     *Annie!* ORDER UP!

We got a mountain, a mountain of somethin' right.
The menu's callin' it *Fruit* but you might say it's *The Light*.
It's only good for *Now* (the greatest item of all we price)
'cause you know that time is money and this one'll cost you life.

But the taste lasts forever and it's served with a sturdy spine
a side of greens and smiles and a chilled piece of mind
a slice of life, toasted lightly, then buttered on one side
and a jug of lime to chase the bite in our famous recycled pride.

So you better get it while it's hot, or you can wait until ya freeze.
But I'ma be out back playin' marbles in the trees.

# OPAL PEOPLE

SHE TOLD ME IT WAS ALRIGHT
TO EXPLODE AND BE FREE
BECAUSE SHE SAW THE PLEASURE REVOLVING ME
BECAUSE THAT'S MY KIND OF ENERGY
BECAUSE I'M AMAZING SHE WAS SAYING
FOR THE THINGS I SEE
AND SHE'S PRETTY AMAZING TO ME
BUT I SAID *I WOULDN'T LOOK CENTERED*
AND *I WOULDN'T BE GROUNDED*
AND *I MIGHT LACK FOCUS*
*WHEN THE PAST COMES TRYING TO STROKE US OFF*
*AND YOU MIGHT SEE THE MISTAKES I MAKE*
*BECAUSE I CAN'T DO ANYTHING*
*WITHOUT GETTING LOST IN IT*
*AND GOING FULL CIRCLE BEFORE I STEP*
SEE THERE'S A VOICE THAT TAKES ME UNDER
BUT SHE KNOWS THE WAY I NEED THE PAIN
SO WE GO INTO THE WORLD OF WONDER
BY THE SYSTEMATIC FLEE OF THESE TERRIFIED FEET
AND SHE STRIPS THOSE THOUGHTS AWAY
AND SOMETIMES, Y'ALL, THIS WON'T MAKE SENSE
BUT *SOMETIMES* AIN'T NO ACCIDENT
BECAUSE VISIONS DON'T DANCE ON THEIR OWN
SO SINCE WE'RE GONNA BE GOIN'
THIS FAR FROM HOME
WE'LL USE WIDE EYES AND CAST OUR PLASTIC SEEDS
TO THOSE WHO LIKE TO PLAY
HACKSAW JIGSAW NAME-THAT-GREED
AND WE'LL GO BOLT-ACTION
TO SICKLE THE STITCHES
AND STEP OUR STAINED GLASS FEET
INTO AN OPAL SKIN
WHERE WE'RE ALLOWED TO EXPLODE
ALL OVER AGAIN
'CAUSE WHEN THE WATER AIN'T WRINKLED
WE DIVE RIGHT IN
AND YOU KNOW WE BREATHE THAT WATER
WHEN IT'S COMING FROM DREAMS
WITH MOUNTAINOUS WAVES OF AMBER IN ITS GRAIN
THAT FLUTTERS LIKE HUMANS

REACHING FOR LIGHT
WHO'VE GOT TEN THOUSAND
POUNDS OF SONGS IN THEIR EYES
AND WE NEVER DARE COME UP FOR AIR
IF WE'RE ONLY HALFWAY THROUGH
'CAUSE THEN WE WOULDN'T LOOK CENTERED
AND WE WOULDN'T BE GROUNDED
AND WE MIGHT LACK FOCUS
AND I'M JUST COMING BACK TO TELL YOU
BEFORE THIS GETS US OFF
SO IF YOU FINALLY MAKE IT
THERE'LL BE A GIANT RUSH OF RIVER
UNDER A GIANT VARNISH CLOUD
IT'LL BE WRAPPED IN GIANT STONES
AND *LOUD*
LIKE SILENCE STANDING OUT
SO PLEASE, TAKE YOUR TIME
WITH THE BUBBLE AND THE JET BLANK STARE
AND REMEMBER WHAT IT TOOK TO GET HERE
BECAUSE IT WON'T BE PAST TENSE HALF-WIT SMOKE
IT'LL BE FLOW-INFLICTED OPAL DROVES
OF THOSE WHO KNOW HOW TO RISE AND GROW
AND HOW TO RESPOND TO THE END OF THE WORLD
*SO*, SHE SAID, *IT'S OKAY TO BE RACING*
*AND IT'S OKAY TO EXPLODE*
*IF THAT'S WHAT IT'S GONNA TAKE*
*FOR YOU TO finally*

*let*

    *it*

      *go.*

30

# I Got Gone

I got gone gone gone. I was throwing my body around
like a wand and they were yelling, *Slow down, boy, slow down!*
But I don't get their rigid rules. How they fold their arms out
like a people who praise while they dawdle in a box
between greed and release

as if
this dawdling speaks for the free
as if
in their praise they're speaking for me.

But it's just talk, y'all
and goddamn can they talk, like a people who say
they're alive while they hurdle by on
backslides, alibis, technicalities, loopholes
                    and a bolt-action judgment.
It's people in an itty bitty box who think
that just because the top's open now
there'll always be a way to get up and fly out
and they'll fly out anytime but
                    now.

But now they've got hate-with-a-smile they'd rather expose
so you better be wearing your expensive clothes because the dark
don't just go through their eyes anymore,
it shows in the way they bury the poor and I don't know
who they are or what they want or where they're coming from

because their skin is so thick and deep I can't tell if they've got hearts
underneath from a complete lack of a rising beat
so I got gone gone gone. I was throwing my body around
like a wand and they where yelling, *Slow down, boy, slow down!*

But I don't get their rigid rules, yelling at me,
*Slow down, boy, slow down. No, speed up! Be first! Don't cut!*
*Get lost! Get found! Get it right! Learn to fly! Jump this high!*
*Stay grounded! Go! Fight! Win! Shut up! Speak up! Sit still!*
*Move out! March! Stop!*

Am I dizzy, God?
*Yeah, you are.*
Yeah, that's what I thought.
Because from outside this box looking in
I see a people who've got old guts, old wits, old thrust and regret

for an old loss on an old goal that clearly began
this fucked-up caged-in maze no God would ever keep us in.
It's a people who got bought out,
shut down, kicked back and meter read
by an old hope in an old scene that we've all been too proud to frame
in our                bones

so I got gone   gone         gone
in a ballroom dance with Leonard Cohen
trading skin tight words in perfect form
around an itty bitty box full of people

being born
yelling at me
screaming,
*Whadaya think you're doin', boy?!*

And I just yelled back,

*Y'all, I'm goin' home*
*for something to ease these fits*

*so I can drift*
*lift*

*instrument.*
*And slow down.*

*Slow*
        *down.*

# FLARE GUNS AND EARTHQUAKES

Because it makes a writer appear self righteous, they say to never
begin a book or a poem with the word *I.* So I didn't.
But you should know, this is about me.

If it comes off as self righteous, that's because I speak from a temple
of twenty percent tithing where too many vandals toting crosses and
scandals have chucked their hymnal pulp so far up into my pit that I
cannot deny it, y'all –
I'm pissed.

I I I mutherfuckers, this poem is about *me,* and some anger, flare
guns and earthquakes and maybe I'm gonna yell, but let that stand
as a warning to all the hyper-critical poets out there who have
condemned yelling or even cussing as a way of *expressing* oneself
through the art of *spoken* word:

I yell sometimes.

If that doesn't fit inside your guidelines, feel free to get up off of your
appropriate-*ness* and fuck off.

I'd be lying if I told you different. I'm ready to kill something. I'll
probably only get as far as my brain cells, but I'm gonna *kill them.*

My smile is being murdered by the church and the state of
surcharges. The courts in Iowa City recently made me pay a $250
"self-observation" fee. I told them I would watch myself for free.
They disagreed. This is a true story.

Keeping the money dogs at bay is like eating rocks on Novocaine.
Soon I will wail. My dogs are barking.

Rich people, I am one Robin-Hooded dream away from stealing
your slave trade diamonds and buying me and *my* crew some loafers
and a massage.

Bank of America charges me eight dollars if I need assistance from
a human being and nearly four dollars when I want to withdraw my
own money but am outside of my state.

Yeah, I'm outside of my state here!

I've got a voice inside my cell phone telling me how to hang up when I'm done with my call! Since the inception of time I have known how to hang up my own phone! And I have *NEVER* needed to dial *POUND* for more options! You're wasting my minutes!
Goddamn it!

They can put a man on the moon but they can't put a voice inside my cell phone to let me know when I'm about to go over the minutes on my minute usage plan just before they start charging me a testicle!

Where red ferns used to grow!
Into giant peaches!

There's your fucking poetry quota!

When poets lose their poetry and their minds this is the kind of entitled crap you're gonna get so start paying my broke ass to write prettier fucking images instead of sandcastles in a colander if you really want me to give you what the gods gave me.

This is my job, and I know it's worth more than a car wreck in a movie. A car wreck in a movie could pay off my financial aid, fill the holes in my teeth, fix the opaque spots in my vision, and still have enough left over for groceries and a goddamned bottle of Xanax.

But instead my stomach works as a 24-hour meat grinder fueled by butterflies and college debts that have since dominoed into eight different papers named Bill who all come over and trash my apartment once a month with treaded water.

And yes, I *know* it was inappropriate to have used the word *poet* or *poetry* in a *poem, Professor,* but it's a little too late for that *now.*

Last week I went to church for the first time this side of freedom. I was hoping to give back the baggage they gave me in exchange for all the tithing but no one was there. Instead it was a letter stapled to the door from the preacher said, "My parishioners now work for the state and I, the preacher, am out being filled with the words of the National Poetry Slam."

34

Y'all, there is an entire congregation who go by the exact same name.
They live inside my ears when I am angry and alone and writing.
If you stood us side by side with a Bible, we would be the ones who
looked blessed. Broke, but blessed. Without the proper fork, sans
writing etiquette and one late payment away from a pawn shop,
but blessed.

This poem may have meant nothing to you but I am confident,
tonight, that my taking the time to actually write out my anger
instead of acting on it has saved the life of at least eleven people in
parking enforcement.

*I,* mutherfuckers. This flawless poem was about me and some anger,
flare guns and earthquakes, and maybe                you.

# Aaron

He's got a two-year-old in his left arm being terribly two.
His wife is nagging relentlessly. I know his name is Aaron
because she begins and ends most every sentence with his name.
I also know that it's spelled A – A – R – O – N
because I can hear the extra A in the dental drill of her voice.
She sends my nerves to war.

The fourth swipe of the food card fails.
This time Aaron puts back the orange juice.
There goes breakfast again and the red on Aaron's face
grows one shade closer to crying.

Though you may feel for him now I am confident
you wouldn't like Aaron
unless the two of you met at a hot rod show sponsored by
crystal meth, invaded personal space, the NRA
and *you* were sincerely having a good time.

Aaron has offended everyone he has ever met
but right now
as he tries to break free from check stand number six
with all his might I can tell
Aaron wants everyone to know he's sorry.

*Aaron, this is why we're on food stamps because you can't count, Aaron.*

She growls at him as if she were being paid good money to do so.
I know he's thought of killing her
or himself
at least twice this week already. Today
it's Monday, and as much as I'd love to believe differently
I don't think Aaron is gonna get out of this life
what he came here for. Not this time around.

His two-year-old son bats him in the face
and squirms like a spiral screaming
downward. Now
follow me here
one more time, from the top, with feeling: I hope

I've already been an ape at every stage of evolution.
Hope I've already been a beautiful woman of color
made to feel ugly for wearing that skin
by men who claimed to be Christian with a straight face.

I hope I've already been every evil element in the dark
half of this whole spectrum, that each one of us has
already met on terms as bad as Nazi and Jew, rich and poor,
the United States and East Timor, that finally
this is the moment we make good
and I hope with all my heart
you'll give me one more minute to come full circle
because even if you don't I will not let up
until I take it all the way around this time. I hope

I invented a drum, set a world record, sculpted birds,
built a skyscraper, a lake, a crop circle and a home.
Hope I danced with my tribe around fire (on peyote, near
the tide). Y'all, I hope I lived at least one lifetime
wherein I did not love buttery pastries *so much*
or that even if I did, I had a really high metabolism.

But the only lives I'm absolutely sure I lived are: Once
I was a child who never felt complete about holding anything
until it was broken. Who got erections from the smell of bleach
and who threw food on the floor bought with six dollars
given to his mother by a pawn shop
in exchange for her high school ring.

In the very next life I was a teenager
who never felt complete about anyone holding him unless
they were broken too. Who got erections from the smell of suicide
and who was kicked out of class for refusing the Pledge of Allegiance.

Then one day, for an entire lifetime, I was Aaron
without enough left in me
to get what I came here shoppin' for.

*Aaron! You're holding up the whole line, Aaron!*

*I don't fucking care about the whole line,*
he tells her, staring straight at me
seeing how I am next in line.

I, startled, realizing who I am and how far I've come
with the hope that this is my very last time around
say back to him,
*Aaron, my friend, I know ya don't mean it*
*but if you do*
*maybe that's the difference between me and you.*

# ALL THE TIME

If I had a dime
for every wise man who lost his wise mind
I'd be willing to buy
the first time each one saw the light

'cause I forget the stages of numb
when I go to where they're coming from
and I forget what tune I was told to hum
but it's right here all the time.

and if I had a dime
for every gunslinger's gold-diggin' plight
I might be willing to buy
a bullet for each one into the light

'cause I forget the stages of numb
but I know'm when I see'm comin' one by one
and I forget which tune I was told to hum
when I remember how to fly

high

right here all the time
unless I leave to use my eyes
I'm right here all the time.
Right here.
All the time.

And you're right there toying with love
by the looks of that oiled-up rubber glove
I'd be willing to bet
you don't know how good it gets

'cause you've become the stages of numb
so busy beating yourself with your tongue
and you forget what tune you were told to hum
but you been hummin' it all the time.

Right here all the time
unless I leave to use my eyes
I'm right here all the time.
Right here.
All the time.

# My Point Forever Endlessly

Over the rainbow
into the sky
far past the pot of gold
and back to you and I.

Here we are again
same feeling in a different sin.
Is it worth it to you?
What did you win today?

I got laid naked in the baker's palm.
I was doing all I could to stay calm
but there were songs, psalms and palms
and I must have read one of them wrong.

You think anyone's on our side?
What about the child we pacified?
Think it wants to fight?
Because we've gotta try and keep it alive.

Stalked by a man in me
I think he sees what I'm trying to be.
I feel a little used
but I got my kicks today.

Why do you do it boy?
You judge it once it's been destroyed.
Well you can make all that noise
but they're looking for a happy voice.

> Then the child said
> to the TV in his head,
> *Why's there always something wrong*
> *every single time I turn you on?*

Boy, what'd you go and do?
Told yourself you couldn't choose
so stop blaming the gods
for what you cut to pieces in you.

I mean laying blame it's all the same.
It's a lot more than what you think
but is it worth it to you
and what did you win today?

My point forever endlessly:
I control this phasing fantasy
right now inside me
let me be what I be.
                                              *You're still fighting.*
                                        *You're still grinding your teeth.*
                              *You're still not moving fast enough forward*
                                            *but you're still after me.*


                                       *You're still talking and talking*
                                     *but you're still in over your head*
                                 *because you still talk and talk by the gallon*
                               *but you still don't wanna burn that padded bed*


        *and you still open wide for salt when it's pouring down your wounds*
                                            *and you still bow to gravity*
                                        *and you're still taking it literally*
                   *and you're still laying down the law but you still don't know*
                                                            *the truth*


                            *and you're still not sure what's happening here*
                                      *because you're still not gonna try*
                                *and you're still addicted to way back when*
                                      *instead of coming back to life*


                                  *and I know ya don't wanna hear it*
                                 *because you still can't stand to see*
                            *and I know you still won't drop your guard*
                              *because I just might knock you free, but*


                                       *my point forever endlessly*
                           *is that you still don't know you're amazing*
                               *you still don't know you're amazing*
                               *you still don't know you're amazing*
                                        *for the things you see.*

# MOVING FORWARD

    …that spiral again.

…you need to know
    I'm not going back down there

    …each time feels like I'm being hogtied
and hassled by a massive pack of wolves
    who stalk children until they finally crack
from the impact of a lack of backbone and tact,
    hit hard by the fact that they're part of the lab
testing one-track maze rat tricky traps,
    mind-mapped onto stacks of kid-you-are-really-
unwelcome-here mats made by unfit fat cats,
    sharp as tacks, with manic depressive fractured hands
convinced by the dick in our system's pants
    that we won't amount to jack. Jack, if they catch you
going down on that gap, buying into that martyr-
    on-a-meat-rack crap on purpose, nervous,
feeling bound and burned into *worthless* before you even tried
    cutting the straps, the whole food chain's
gonna laugh at how fast you will pass unnoticed.

    …Do not die in the way you will not let go
of that fully automatic intent to grow
    into perfect
perfect

    perfect…

# A Little Ditty Called Happiness

That boy
sits on a log
eatin' pie
drinkin' fog
playin' fetch
with a dog
that just won't
run his way.

His girl
sits in a swing
that don't sway
singin' songs
about history
and wonders
*Why does vanity
look so good on me?*

And Ma & Pa
are callin' all, sayin',
*Get on down
to yer doctor's mall
he's got a special
on boobs and lips
and butts
and cake*

while cousin's on
the cellular phone
callin' more talk shows
for the folks at home
who've got opinions
on solutions
for the problems
that ain't their own and

let's hear it for the high
class killin' Winnie-the-Pooh
with the molds they cast
in this clash of titans
that no longer remains
in check
'cause Superman
broke his neck.

But there's a
little ditty called Happiness, says
I'm gonna walk away from this
before I lose my masterpiece
to an Etch-A-Sketch again

and in the mornin'
when I rise
if everybody's really bein'
randomly kind and if
I can feel as good
as I do tonight
then I'm gonna walk
away from this

with a little ditty
called Happiness

but...

religion's paced
the rats in this race
for a low fat succulent
jumbo shake
while a man in the street
like an old pile of meat
buys groceries from
the local aluminum can

and as they juggle his balls
with tightened fists
in a world war
on the streets of wit
the president eats
the smiles from our cheeks
puckers up and
he waves his hands

and…

Ma & Pa
they're callin'
all sayin', *Get on back*
*to yer doctor's mall.*
*He's got a special*
*on computer chips*
*for the brains*
*in our kids*

while some drunk fool
with a class at school
blows sawdust
off his power tools
and looks down
a row of the dummies
he's created
again.

But there's a
little ditty called Happiness, says
I'm gonna walk away from this
before I lose my masterpiece
to an Etch-A-Sketch again

and in the mornin'
when I rise
if they vacuum up the gun smoke
out of the sky
if we will love ourselves
despite the crimes
if we will drop our jaws at fire

when it's flyin' out our eyes
and right now
all come back to life
and if
I can feel as good
as I do tonight
then I'm gonna walk
away from this

with a little ditty
called Happiness.

LIVE
FOR
A
LIVING

# WORKS FROM
## *LIVE FOR A LIVING*
## 2004-2007

---

*For experiencing this moment
without craving any other answer
than exactly what is happening.*

# THE INFORMATION MAN

After over four-hundred thousand miles, twelve dozen breakdowns
nervous, one too many midnights and a whole bunch of broken laws
later, I have come here from out of the rain and into this rest area,
caught twenty-two miles between you and me, watching the
Information Man behind his information booth, juggling predictable
conversation with folks who look like iceberg lettuce and who believe
that somehow the flat lines of small talk will give us life.
I want them to leave

like a big deal orchestra removing itself from the string section
so I can fiddle with fate and make music.

There is a distance the size of bravery.
It forms like words in the mouth of a baby reaching out for the point
where all things meet. On one end of it sits an Information Man
who I imagine holds down his second job as church bartender behind
locked doors leading to a bell tower we will never get to see
                                                    sinners.

At the other end of this space I am standing like shoe polish
on an overstocked shelf hoping that one day someone will pick me
to make things better.

This is not a showdown or a shootout. We are not facing off.
But I can feel the rumble between dusk and dawn as if the chance
to come clean with myself will be outlawed unless I relax.

I have heard that if you pull a bent breath through the second hole
of a harmonica tuned to the key of Georgia while a train moves by
on the tail end of dusk, there is a good chance you will finally know
                            what it means to rest.

I... have not yet rested.

It takes a long time
to make love with someone
who hated themselves.

It feels like I've been standing here for exactly that long when at last
the rain outside drops off
takes everyone in this rest area with it
except for me                                             and the Information Man

and that's got me thinking: tonight I will get the answer. And you
*know* what I'm talking about – *The* answer. Emphasis on *The* answer.

So I put my best foot forward and take the kind of deep breath
that gives me away as someone who deals with anxiety
and odd numbers every other other every minute.

In between it, the Information Man's eyes grab me then shift
back and forth like mopping floors with the sweat I sweat in battles
against myself. He's got me locked in and is smiling.

If you've never been rocked back by the presence of purpose
this poem is too soon for you. Return to your mediocrity,
plug it into an amplifier and rethink yourself.

Because some of us are on fire for the answer.

I am ready for your little rejection and rebirthing balance in my
stutter steps when the info guy finally pipes up like C.R. Avery
on a piano box
                        and says to me,

*Listen…*

*if I didn't have so much*
*of this life all wrong*
*I would have gotten it right by now.*

*I talk a whole bunch*
*but I really only know a few things*
*so I'm not saying to follow along verbatim here.*

*I'll just tell you the things I tell myself.*
*The things I know.*
*You can see what sticks.*

*I know our shoes*
*were stitched*
*from songs about highways.*

*The best songs*
*are the ones about Georgia*
*even though I've never been there.*

*It's the only place*
*I still believe in Jesus.*

*I know no matter what it is*
*you believe in, you have to spare yourself*
*the futility of making fun of God*

*because that guy*
*hasn't even talked*
*in like          ever.*

*I know troubleshooting yourself in the foot*
*and acting as center of your own universe*
*is a tricky dichotomy to deal with*

*but yes, you are the center*
*of the universe. If you weren't*
*you wouldn't be here.*

*So as the middle of space and everything*
*floating in it, it is your job to know*
*that the emptiness*

*is just emptiness. That the stars*
*are just stars, and that the flying rocks*
*fuc... Really hurt.*

*So please*
*stop inviting all these walls*
*into wide open spaces.*

*I know everything is out there.*
*That's why they call it everything.*

I know there are times
you will lay your head to rest
you will have a moment of brilliance

that grows into a perfect order of words
but you're gonna fall asleep
instead of painting it down on paper.

When you wake up, you will have forgotten
the idea completely and miss it like a front tooth
but at least you know how to recognize

moments of brilliance
because even at your worst
you are fucking incredible.

It comes honest.
So return to yourself
even if you're already there

because no matter where you go
or how hard you try
or what you do

the only person you're ever
gonna get to be
and I know it

thank God
God
God

is you.

# MY TOWN INTRO

My town is cute. Like a bumper sticker. Like Christians
when they sport *Power of Pride* bumper stickers.
What is it you don't understand
about pride being a deadly sin?

My town is cute like *God Bless America* bumper stickers.
Judging by our excessive luxuries
those stickers really work.
Now if we can just get God to bless the whole world.

Alix Olsen's bumper sticker reads:
*I love my country. I just think we should start seeing other people.*

But my town doesn't see other people. We're just too cute.
Like the difference between what we say and what we do
like the fact that violence in any form
is sanctioned by the government as criminal or insane
unless they're the ones who commit it.

My town is cute like people who still shop at Wal-Mart
and claim to be patriotic. Stop it.

My town is cute in the way we worry about the gays
screwing up our family values and the sanctity of marriage
yet we still let our children watch television shows like *Wife Swap,
The Bachelor, Who Wants to Marry a Millionaire, American Idolatry*
and *Fox News.*

My town is so cute that – check this out, y'all:
once – *one time*, five years ago, there were some brown people...
                                        (*boogity boogity*).
They attacked two of our tallest buildings
and killed a boat load of our innocent citizens
kinda like we did, remember,

in Guatemala, Nicaragua, Panama, El Salvador, Tanzania,
Mozambique, Vietnam, Afghanistan, Hiroshima, Philippines,
Kosovo, Bolivia, Angola, Argentina, Brazil, Chile, Dresden,
Dominican Republic, Cuba, Haiti, Indonesia, East Timor,
Cambodia, Iraq, Iraq, Iraq…What the hell are we doing with Israel?

And my cute town pretends we never saw it or had it coming
so in a perpetual attempt to save cute face
we've waged a war on terror about as effective as the war on drugs.

My town is cute when we wage these wars in the name of God,
when we kill each other in the name of the indestructible source
of love.

As many as twenty percent of the polar bears on the Northern Ice
Cap are hermaphrodites due to PCB's being dumped into the ocean.
You won't hear about it on the news because it's too cute,
like a wolf giving birth through its penile canal.

My town is cute like a three-hundred pound tumor
manifesting hair and teeth inside of it
grown from the body
of a two-hundred-and-ten-pound agoraphobic woman.

My town is cute like competitive poetry, the history of Scientology,
plastic surgery and refined sugars.
Like a man swallowing an eight ball of cocaine,
jumping from a five story building to escape police,
then getting up and running away from it all,
y'all, this
is a true story.

The first time my town saw the sky
it sucker punched us in the throat,
left us breathless, said

*I'm gonna keep you awake some nights*
*without touching you.*
*You'll make it up, the pain. You always do.*

# MY TOWN

The first time my town saw the sky / it sucker punched us in the throat / left us breathless / said / *I'm gonna keep you awake some nights / without touching you / You'll make it up / the pain / You always do*

Now my town only buys drowsy formula sky

Otherwise it gets too big / the sky / like when we were three / before we realized / we have balls / The sky does not / Therefore / we have bigger balls than the sky / Please do not talk to us about being tea-bagged by upside down hot air balloons

Where rational conversations and big pictures are concerned / we have no time for getting wrapped up / We are not little presents for your sky / We are just right / Far right / and cute / like three-year-olds / like the book about bunny suicides / cute like Old Yeller / just before he got shot in the rabies / A good actor / that dog

My town was born way off the mark / Sometimes we see it coming / the mark / so we shoot it / with spit wads / or / precision-guided phallic symbols

Every time there is talk of war / people give me reasons why / their town will be bombed first / It's a souped-up sense of self importance bucko / Everybody knows my town / will be bombed first / because once / we planned the construction / of a nuclear power plant / right here in the same fields / where our military children / now carry out covert orders / to keep the word *dumb* alive

Religion / has a hard time working here / It makes us believe that / even when we are alone / someone is watching us / and judging us

Now we're all narcissists / We have a habit of giving / other peoples' gifts to ourselves / but at least our children / still get their confidence booster shots / while our fathers / perform voice reduction surgery / to keep our pleas for help / mime-sized / while our mothers / are bending infinity in half /so that our families / can continue to talk in circles / while we all burn our tongues / when we drink hot cocoa / for the same reason / everybody here / wants to hug the ocean / because it's just / so much

My town knows that / there is something so big / inside all of us / we have to suck / just to distract you / from being directly overwhelmed / by our *real* power / the kind of power that makes you smile / Everybody knows that smiling / is for little girls / the gays / and certain kinds of fish / who are smiling by accident

The shortcuts / my town has taken / have gotten us so far ahead of ourselves / we've actually fallen behind

We would have been better off / learning to herd turtles / into bomb shelters / on a moments notice / giggling at the fact / that we will all / now / die

And it's gonna happen / so fast / we will have never been anything / but really cute / like our three-year-olds / who use folding chairs / to beat lambs / within inches of their lives

Funny thing about that / my town / is inches tall

It's why the sky looks down on us / wants to tell us something / like *grow up* / or *reach up* / or *look up* / *and watch me winking* / *I'm trying* / *to talk* / *to you*

The Earth is traveling / at 66,641mph / around the sun

It simultaneously rotates on itself / at over 1,000mph

My town / it's having / some trouble

sleeping

# FLOCKPRINTER

*Flockprinting is an aggressive electrostatic action using severe heat to force finely chopped fibers onto patterns of fabric, ultimately resulting in soft touch.*

When they told you that this
was your assignment
you flockprinted straitjackets
and suits of armor
so I asked if you wanted to trade jobs
because damn baby, *that* is poetry.

And yeah, these arms fell backwards
when ya did it. Chest outstretched,
open to the way you palms-up turn me.

I knew you'd be good.
I just didn't know how good.

Even before we met, when the assignment was
to draw words with their own literal meanings
I would write out each letter of the word *love*
using winning halves of wishbones, melted Crayons
and the toe tips of the great dancers
who've quit dancing
because I don't give up on shit like that.

I always knew I'd find you.

Even before we met, when the assignment was
to partner up in ice water and keep our heads above it
I'd watch boys with girls take the shallow
end of the eighth grade like suckerfish
swapping skin deep aquarium air tubes, trying to make
each other's shivers fit.

We don't swim that way. Never gonna.
Flockprinter, you

have been a long time coming
and the clouds have rolled you in slowly
but I ain't mad at the upshot sky.

Rain, it's my lucky number.
It's the author of release.
It taught me monsters are easy to come by
so I went out and found the beast

before we met, when the assignment was
to incomplete myself with sad songs
and recycled insults, when I was spun out, eyes
bagged teeth fist first in lust and considering Jesus.

You were there.
You have been the whole journey
and I ain't got nothin' against goin' home
to you

Flockprinter

you look good in your tidal wave,
toe-to-toe with the mean blue moon,
head raised up like a lighthouse.

You are buttercups spraying out the mouths of doves,
fireworks stuck in the air. You're a freestanding landing pad
held together by choir claps. You're a god not afraid
to walk with the saviors who ride monkeys
around on their backs, kicking up mercury,
spreading upward openly, carrying breath          well.

You're an eighteen-stringed guitar, heart
sparkin' off of roots dancing out of the river's edge.
You walk like a free country with an affinity for thick skin.
You live humming to the tune of let loose like a railway
banging through the middle of Novocain, an open-winded
underwater fire escape.

Flockprinter

you have, now are, and always will be
my reflection of individuality
carried out by the acoustic drift
of a snowflake
living with a fingerprint.

And I am rumble motion jawbone
waterlogged with ink spots
smiling ear to ear
armed with backbone and busted zoo gates
promising you
from the bottom of my harmonica pocket
forever
you will never have another lonely holiday.

Even now, where the assignment is
to live without a destination
I end up with you
and the rain
released

both
flockprinting stars
between me and the beast.

# TWIN BLUE HIGHWAY HEAD

Dear March 13, 2007,

It's 4:46am in the Seattle airport waiting on a plane. No sleep yet.
I am paying close attention to people and typing into my phone.

*[cursor]*
*[cursor]*
*[cursor]*
*[cursor]*
*[cursor]*

We are on orange alert.
David Lynch wrote a movie called *This Morning*. I am in it. A lot.

At the men's room I walked in on a timid, puffy-eyed pale kid
standing confused under the fluorescent light in front of the mirror
using his jaw to pull his jaw off. That didn't work so he mashed his
lips into each other and around. He was pretending to not be startled
by my entry. He was slow to the startle. He felt so goddamned sad.

There is one thin single-spaced exceedingly long line for expensive
bagels and coffee and hardly anyone else in the airport. They're all
just standing there three gates long, mooing, quietly. I'm loud hungry
inside but the thought of standing with them makes no sense to me.

To get here I ran down the escalator by myself without looking up
at that stupid window from where people wave goodbye. Today I
believe in ghosts.

*[cursor]*
*[cursor]*
*[cursor]*

I've found as much love for airports as I have for myself.
And as much hate.

On cue the guy next to me dials his phone and says to someone at the other end, *This is a voice from your past.*

I miss his voice. I miss him so goddamn much.

Fluorescent Fixture,

Flicker

# GIANT SAINT EVERYTHING

There were days I wanted out.
But then you would go and do things
like dive into the Vancouver ocean,
big brilliant cliché poem that you are,
water rolling off your back
as you swam toward a sunset
that hung like a sacred recipe
painted all the way around your holy head.

And then there were the ways you watched me
moving back into my cave where the wheels turn,
same wheels that drove you off.

I should have told you before talking in terms of *forever*
that any given day wears me out and works me sour,
that there are nights when the sky is so clear
I stand obnoxious underneath it
begging for the stars to shoot me
just so I can feel at home.

What's left of you now is a shrine
built from the pieces I kept of your presence,
your incredible stretch of presence. It sits in our room
like a sandpiper, cross-legged and crying
remembering the night we met
and the day you left
and the Light
shifting in between.

By the side of it stands a picture of the poem
where I promised
you will never have another lonely holiday.

The words *I promise* and *forever*
begged me not to use them
but sometimes I don't listen to God
so you can imagine how much it hurt
to let your last birthday pass
with no word.

On August third
you weren't the only one
comin' up lonesome. Listen

if I had to make a list of everything everywhere
the very last to-do
on that infinite list
of every single thing
would be
to hurt you

so I need you to know
that in an attempt to keep my promise
I did write a letter to you on your birthday.

It was covered in stickers of flock-printed stars,
choir claps and a bonfire of buttercups stuck in the air
but when I finally drew enough courage to send you
all the love in the world, my hand
snapped off in the mailbox
from clenching.

It was returned to me
with a gospelstitch, a hope stamp
and a note etched into the palm I had to pry open
with the pressure of pitching doves
reminding me
we agreed to let each other go.

There is a point when tears don't work
to wash things away anymore.
Grabbing for breath has broken my fingers.
I miss you so much some days
I beg for the airplane to crash
with just enough time in the free fall
for scribbling *I love you* across my chest.

That way, when they find my burning breast plate,
they will tell you how the very last thing I did with my life
was call out your name.

Arnold Remond Liesting

I know your momma didn't raise a sissy
so it's best if I believe that you've bounced back
and been born again, but baby, in the bottom left
corner of dreams, in the dark spot where it gets
windy and hollow, I can still see you

flailing
eating knuckle cake
full torque and tender
heart pounding from being
pulled under
feet bleeding from bracing
for endings
tongue dying to curse
*forever*

because promises murder us backwards
when people like me don't keep them.

And yes, we all deserve absolution.
But especially you. You and Faith,
you've got the same hunger punch,
same song, still rising off the water train
running through the laws
of a moon dead set on daylight
digging marbles from the trees
in a love not scared to make no sense
but still man enough to see
the same devastating reason for living this life,
my Giant Saint Everything.

*Forever.*
*I Promise.*

These words have buckled my lips
so far back to the beginning
that I am now only allowed today.

So today, from my snap-chested heart spraying
fully flying, sending out the birds,
today I stop believing in words.

Today all my visions reverted to blurs
like the night we saw the light
and I could not shut up
but I swear
I was feeling silence.

# GANDHI'S AUTOBIOGRAPHY

Gandhi's Autobiography is on my pillow.
I put it there every morning after making my bed
so I'll remember to read it before falling asleep.
I've been reading it for six years.
I'm on Chapter Two.

Gary Necci gave me a book when he left my house one time.
I don't remember the name of it exactly
but I think it was called something like, *Kid
You are Seriously Co-Dependent.*
He thought I might wanna flip through and learn about that.
I feel like it's more important to finish Gandhi's autobiography first,
Gary.

I keep forgetting to put *focus* on my to-do list.
I keep forgetting to wander and have fun.
I know I'm transparent
but my insecurities are in all the right places
so go ahead, have a look.

When I was a child, the first thing I would do
upon entering someone's home
is ask them where they kept the toys.
If they said that they didn't have any toys I'd be like,

*What the fuck?!*

When I was a child
I would chase my babysitter around the house
viscerally sounding out the end of the letter *L*
*llllllllll. Lllllllllllllllllll! Uhl. Uhl. Uhlll ull
llllllll.* She thought it was weird.

Mom had bought me a big cylinder can of alphabet blocks
with different colored letters of the alphabet
painted on each side. I had convinced myself I swallowed
the yellow letter L. I was trying to get it out of my body.
My babysitter never came back.

There are so many things I want to get out of my body.
When will we own ourselves completely?
Tell me what it is you want me to own and I will take it.
Damaged goods? You bet.
Hit or miss? No doubt about it.
Misses important social cues?

                                        Pretty often.


I'm dirty underneath the light,
pale on the backside of my bright
and I feel so silly about learning a language
whenever I experience God
because that guy
is so                    fast.

My best friend can speak six languages.
I still get excited English took hold.

Sometimes I don't feel
like I'm doing my part on this planet.

Sometimes I read without paying attention
hoping everything will just sorta sink in
so that if I ever do need the answers, ya know,  like on a test,
my subconscious will somehow pull through for me.

I talk too much.
If you see me being quiet
don't ask me what's wrong.
I'm just practicing.

I often wonder if anyone died
because of the pencil I handed to a prisoner
at San Quentin State Penitentiary.
He stuck it in his pocket.
The point is
there are things wrong with us. Maybe.
There are things wrong with me. Clearly.

But I do have the ability to split epiphanies
with my face on demand. Hold me
like a birthmark. Awkward if you have to.

I wander
so if you lose me
don't worry.

After the big tsunami, the only structure still standing
in the wiped out village of Malacca
was a statue of Mahatma Gandhi.
I wanna be able to stand like that.
Even after getting gargled and spanked and spit out by God

I wanna know that I do not have to fall
every time the sky opens up like a coin return
to change me
into little lines on maps
drawing circles around my blood
to show the scars
                here
in the shape of Gandhi on my pillow
to show that I've been here before and tonight
is not the last time
we will see the light.

# AIR HORN

And when the rain

dropped into us another song

we went along

we played a long

tambourine

shaped like a tree made out of bones

I shook the sound

and climbed the song

until a string

tied to a cloud we all called home

it moved along

and I held on.

# Bedrooms And Battle Scars

As best as I can remember
this is how it happened:

There was a tree at the bottom of a cornfield
where I hid from people who lived inside my house.
I called them stepsisters and fathers
but they were monsters
holding out for light.

They were people who did not know what they were holding out for.
They did not intend to be so beastly and wounded.
They wanted to cross over into the way I wander
but they could not find me
and I paid for that.

In 1974, I was born. The next three years were a bit of a blur
understandably so
though my mother has repeatedly
reminded me I was a loud baby.

I wobbled and sucked my thumb, marveled and opened up,
crapped my pants, cute as the next kid, and my cheeks
could be used for sailing.

But in 1978 my mom's car broke down. We were brutally
rescued by a truck driver for eight years. He had the hell
inside of him. Rug burn. I know because
he pulled me across the floor.

One day Mom decided it was not okay anymore that he kept
falling into other women's va-who-who's,
so we left him
realizing
we had not actually been rescued
all them years ago.

In those days I jumped six feet from my light switch to my bed
in order to avoid the hands of anything underneath it.
There are still dents in my shins
because I didn't always hit the mattress.

Bedrooms and battle scars
both keep well in the dark.
Hard dark.

In the sunken-eyed sector of a nightmare
paved with uppercuts
and heart sparks
spark plugs
and fist
first
release.

Listen.
I'd fall in love with you
if you would beat these people out of me.

# Human The Death Dance

On the face of her phone, Wileen programs a message to herself
so that when the alarm clock rings the screen flashes,

> *EVERY DAY IS ONE DAY LESS.*
> *EVERY DAY IS ONE DAY LESS.*

For some people, happiness is just
a reduction in suffering. Like Jordan.
Jordan tattoos the words

> *FORGIVE ME*

in thick black letters down the inside of his arm
so that when he looks at his wrist
he will remember to not hate himself so much.
What they both keep forgetting
is that there is life after survival.

When Dave left, Mary started
sticking her face between the film projector
and the movie screen
so that when the credits roll
she still gets to be somebody.

When Tara's past comes back
she mashes chalk into the sidewalk
until her knuckles bleed.
She scribbles and scrapes, scribbles and scrapes
until the words take shape and this is what they say:

> *I wanna die mutherfuckers*
> *die DIE mutherfuckers*
> *hold tight if I love ya*
> *'cause it might not last long.*

Y'all, we're all gonna die.
That's the exciting part.
It's learning how to live for a living
there's the tricky stitch.

74

Just ask Denise, whose family taught her
when she came into this world
that family equals love
so Denise took that shit seriously
but after a lifetime of craving acceptance from their cruelty
she now finds herself jamming Polaroid pictures
of these people into her typewriter
and pounding out the last letter of the word *mercy*
over and over and over again.
She strikes the key Y.

*Y? Y? Y?! Y?! Y?!*

And the answer,
the answer comes
in the form of a handwritten letter
from the moon,
says,

> *This*
> *is brutally beautiful. So are we.*
> *This*
> *is endless. So are we.*
> *We*
> *can heal this.*
>
> *Signed,*
>
> *Crater Face*
> *P.S. See me for who I am.*
> *We've got work to do.*

But my father, he didn't read moon,
he didn't speak moon, and he didn't write moon
so there was no note left next to his body
when he chose to leave this world on purpose
without telling us where he was going or why.

There are still days you can catch me tape recording
eternal silence
and playing it backwards for an empty room
just so I can listen to his dying wish, *shhhhhhhh.*

Yes.
It's true.
And the apple
doesn't fall too far from the tree
but thank goodness my family tree
was in an orchard on a hill
that rolled me to the river
and that river
ripped me through the rapids
and those rapids
rushed me
into this moment
right here
right now
with you
at the mouth.

Y'all, this is my church.
And if church is a house of healing,
Hallelujah
Welcome
Come on in
as you are.
*Exactly* as you are.
Have a look around.

Stay out of my porn.

There are massive stacks of bad choices in my backyard.
Clearly I have not yet reached enlightenment beyond
a few fleeting moments, but I'm trying
and I found something here I want you to have.
It's not much. It's just a story but it's all I've got
so take it. It's called *Dillon*.

Dillon's drug of choice was more
so he took more and more and more
until the day he woke up babbling
in a pool of his own traffic jam
realizing he was killing off the best parts of himself
and claiming he could read people's skin.
When Dillon looked down at his heart flap, it read

*Boy, go find your spine*
*and ride it outta here.*

Wileen's gut said

*Day 1.*

Jordan's arms were

*FULLY FORGIVEN.*

Mary's face

*The*
*Endless.*

Tara's knuckles healing.

Denise's fingertip typing *C.*

*C. C. C! C! C!*

And my smile. Dillon said
my smile said *Fix it*
so I came back here to the mouth of the river
to look at my own reflection
under the moonlight
and see what it says for myself
where down my whole body
it is written

*P.S. See me for who I am.*
*We've got work to do.*

As for Crater Face,
I don't speak for that guy.
His skin
is a brutally beautiful
handwritten letter
from the sun.

# HEALING HERMANN HESSE

Hermann wants to eat nicotine sometimes. He asks
for a lot. He paces space to make himself nervous
because some people are better at surviving than
living. If you wanna get heavy he'll teach you. He
knows it. Spends his time falling from the weight.
Got a lead brain. It's a battle magnet. He carries it
around by the guilt straps. Don't laugh. You didn't
see the size of the blizzard that birthed him. Fits
of snow. Cotton rocks. Whipped white bullet stretches
pinned with chips of teeth to his habit of crying for help.
He doesn't land well. Hates landing. It reminds him of not
living up.

Listen.
I know there were days you wanted to die.

Days you misplaced all the right words then waited
to make sense once everyone here stopped watching.

Nights you let them beat up your body in bed
because redemption was still alive in you howling.

Uncompromising.
Gathering strength.

Happiness
is too far to fall.

Felt like ecstasy
when they pounded it out of you.

Those days of dead weather high strung out together
and spoke for you.

You told everyone here it was a good life,
smiled and waved back into the wails of your wind fight,

into the parts of the past that haunt you,
all the days you weren't being yourself.

78

It's why most of the past
still haunts you,

Milk Worder,
Mr. Self Murder.

Hiding is not an option for people
so good at showing up. You show up.

It is okay that you showed up missing.
We've all abused ourselves

then looked over
the wrong shoulder about it.

Call it Fatherlock.
You were picked like this.

I know you hate the hope.
It's all the hope that makes you stay.

And you stay so far off the ground.

Hermann will not bow down to gravity. Falling
he catches up to himself midair just before the ground
smacks. *Pullthroat,* they call'im. *Sharp turner.* Nothing
touches the ground here.  Ground is at capacity.
He sees that. He falls back. He patches parachutes
together with a kite knife.  It's big enough to raise him
in the updrafts where he hides himself away in the angles
of air outlined by his knack for believing that this life
is gonna work itself out.

# THE ART OF DIE SMILINGLY

If you really want this
to be your last day on Earth
on purpose
and there will be children
who are yours
and you will be leaving them
permanently
please
before you go
taking away mother nature's chance
to translate you properly
listen
right now
with no doubts
head out
hire hard working
lovers of life
who really need the money.
They may be difficult to find
but they are worth it.
Pay them well.
They will build you
the world's largest neon sign.
If you don't have the money
steal it from someone
who kills people with it.
If you get busted
fuck it
it's not like you had better plans.
Don't tell anyone
what you are doing.
You do not need
to leave a note.
The workers will hang your sign
from the deepest edge
of a grand canyon
where you will wait
until dawn
in stillness

for the low
down
fog.
Now duck back into that.
There will be a rocket pack.
Pick it up.
Put it on.
Dry your eyes.
Bend down.
Feel around
for the beaded metal
pull string
leading to the neon sign.
Hold it in your hand.
Say a thank you
to anything.
Run
fast as you can
for canyon gravity.
No last words.
Just jump
high
up
and out
as you quick
flip the switch
to the booster pack.
Pull the string
to light the sign.
Open wide
your ending life
and hang on tight to the lifting
because you may
shoot up and outward
as the neon writes its light
through the night
in cursive tubes of waterslides
hung high and bright
on the canyon side says
*DON'T WORRY KIDS*
*THE MOON WILL CATCH ME!*

There will be a blast of fire
in the eyes of the workers watching.
Dust will spread out
like a helicopter castle
when it's landing
even though you're leaving.
Your children will be below
in awe of you
waiting
and wondering
*Dad, what*
*are you doing?*
Jetpacks have parachutes.
Power off.
Fall into it.
Fall any way you want to.
Saving yourself
is jarring.
Look around
on the way back down.
You're not the only piece of patchwork
birds can pull worms from.
If I were the man in the moon
and my eyes were a little better
I would barely
be able to make out
the words
stretched
across
your parachute top
stitched by the lovers of life
who are very good with signs like
*DON'T WORRY MOON*
*THE KIDS WILL CATCH ME.*

# GUITAR REPAIR WOMAN

My mother told me,
*If you ever become a rock star*
*don't smash the guitar.*
*There are too many other poor kids out there*
*who have nothing*
*and they see that nonsense*
*when all they wanna do is play that thing.*
*Boy, you better let them play.*

If she ever starts in on one of these lectures
your best bet is to pull up a chair, chief
'cause Momma don't deal in the abridged version.

She worries about me so much some days
it feels like I'm watching windshield wipers
on high speed
during a very light sprinkle
and I gotta tell'er, *MOM.*
*YOU ARE MAKING ME NERVOUS.*

She was born to be laid back, y'all, I swear
but some of us were brought up in households
where *carefree* is a stick of gum, or a panty liner,
and the only option for getting out is to walk faster.

That woman can run. In high heels. Backwards.
While double checking my homework, bursting
my bubble, rolling enough pennies to make sure
that I have lunch money, and preparing for a meeting
at my school on her only day off so she can tell
Mrs. Goss the music teacher,

*If you ever touch my boy again, big lady,*
*I'll bounce a hammer off your fingers.*

I remember her doing these things swiftly
and with a smile in discounted thrift store
business suits that she wore just bright
and distinguished enough to cover up
thirty years of highway scars truckin'
through her spine. Some accidents
you don't need to see, rubbernecker.
Keep movin'
because she made it.
She's alive
and she's famous.

We can stretch Van Gogh paintings on billboards
from Kilgore, TX to Binghamton, NY
and you still won't find the brilliant brush strokes
it takes to be a single mother, sacrificing
the best part of her dreams to raise a baby boy
who, on most days,
she probably wants to strangle.

We disagree *a lot*. For instance: Mom still thinks
it's okay to carry on a conversation
full throttle
at 7 a.m.
whereas I think...
Oh, I don't think at 7 in the morning!

But we both agree that love makes no mistakes
so at night time, when she's winding down
and I'm still writing books about how to get comfortable
in this skin she gave me,
I see rock stars on stages smashing guitars
and it is then I wanna find them a comfortable chair
get them a snack
and introduce them to daylight...

This is my mother.

Tresa B. Olsen

Runner of the Tight Shift
Taker of the Temperature
Leaver of the Light On
Lover of the Underdog
Mover of the Mountain
Winner of the Good Life
Keeper of the Hope Chest
Guitar
                    Repair
                              Woman

and I am her son.

Buddy Wakefield.

I play a tricked-out electric pen
thanks to the makers of music and metaphor
but I do my best to keep the words in check
and I use a padded microphone
so I don't hurt you
because sometimes, I smash things
and I don't ever wanna let her down.

# GENTLEMAN
# PRACTICE

BY **BUDDY WAKEFIELD**

# WORKS FROM
## *GENTLEMAN PRACTICE*
### 2007–2011

*This book is for people who keep thinking their work is done; people who've yet to break through the rest of the resistance, who aim to thrive, but still get stuck in the excuse. Don't stop arriving. You're almost there. You know the clearing is just ahead. I know because we are happening at the same time.*

*This book is for people who keep showing up to support someone else unfolding, to bear witness to themselves, to see if something true of heart will happen.*

# WE WERE EMERGENCIES

We can stick anything into the fog,
make it look like a ghost.
But tonight let us not
become tragedies. We are not funeral
homes with propane tanks in our windows
looking like cemeteries. Cemeteries are just
Earth's way of not letting go.                    Let go.

Tonight let's turn our silly wrists
so far backwards
the razor blades in our pencil tips
can't get a good angle on all that beauty inside.

Step into this
with your airplane parts.
Move forward
and repeat after me with your heart:

*I no longer need you to fuck me*
*as hard as I hated myself.*

Make love to me
like you know I am better
than the worst thing I ever did.
Go slow. I'm new to this.

But I have seen nearly every city in the world
from a rooftop
without jumping. I have realized
that the moon did not have to be
full for us to love it, that we are
not tragedies stranded here beneath it,
that if my heart really broke
every time I fell from love
I'd be able to offer you confetti by now.

But hearts don't break.
They bruise and get better.
We were never tragedies.

We were emergencies.
Go ahead. Call 9-1-1.
Tell them I'm having a fantastic time.

# Let It Go

Let's let go from the get go.
Let go let god let it go.
Leave it alone.
Let it pass.
Let it be.
Laissez-faire.
C'est la vie.
What's done is done.
Hang up on it.
Land the plane.
Don't get on that train.
The bus has already left.
This too shall pass.
Shake it off.
Cut your losses.
Bust loose.
Break free.
It's water under the bridge.
What comes around goes around.
Go around.
Get over it.
Get it together.
Get a grip.
Get moving.
Keep moving.
Move on.
Move forward.
Forward.
March.
Stop.
Drop it.
Squash it.
Please.
Release.
Relax.
Spilled water cannot be poured back.
Do not look back.
Enough is enough.
Stand down.

Stay still.
Be quiet.
Yield.
Quit dwelling.
Forget it.
Forgive it.
Give it a rest.
Right now.
As is.
You will be given back the years that the locusts have taken.
Nothing is against us.
Our cravings for annihilation will be laid to rest
with the apocalyptic resentment
and the compounding stress
and *Yes* said the answer.
*Yes* said the breath.
*The consequences are immediate*
*so when you breathe*
*you might try freeing both lungs up.*

# HOME

Remember when you were four years old and your room
looked like a war zone so Mom insisted you would be
doing nothing with the rest of your life until it was clean?

Every last puzzle piece, every toy part, every game component.
All the action figures and clothes, reposition the stuffies, make
the bed, including the top bunk, which is a bitch for four-year-olds.
Remember? You took one look, said *no,* then threatened to run away.

So Mom helped you pack. Dead of winter. She got ya
bundled up and zipped into that same puffy jacket all us poor
kids had - the one that looked like navy blue tires stacked on top
of each other, triangle rip in the sleeve. She tucked that scratchy yarn
scarf around your neck, the one MeMaw made, the one you were
allergic to, remember, then she handed you a scary anecdote about
hitch-hiking and scooted you out the front door. Shut it. Locked it.

Remember how fired up you got?

Those puffy red cheeks ready to speak your piece in the name
of everything dinnerlessed and unfaired. You were gonna tell her
a thing or two just before she calmly closed the blinds as well.
Remember that? And remember each weighted pause as you
heavy-stepped it down the frozen front porch cursing this
wicked woman who just so happened to make a fantastic
macaroni and cheese?

But you stuck to your guns and you ran away into the long, cold
winter. For ten minutes. To the edge of the driveway.
Where you realized at four years old
there is no other destination than home.

I remember seeing your exhale blow back across the driveway.
Remember how fast you ran for the house with all your heart
flailing in the epiphany, ready to reveal a changed mind, how you
shoved your whole life through the front door as they opened it, ran
to take center of the living room, planted yourself,

looked everybody right in the eyes, expecting some warm reunion
when you told them you had come to a different decision and would
now in fact be cleaning up the war zone you had created, but no one
said anything except a very disappointed

*Oh… We thought you ran away.*

Remember that?

That moment is responsible for my hate and my sense
of humor. You can call me an angry ghost when I'm gone
or laugh into my disposition, but my mom will still see me
as her wide-eyed wanderer out behind the garage inventing
ways to fend off dog attacks that will probably never happen.

I picked the scabs from my knees because Mom said
it would leave a scar.

*Awesooome!*

# Rapid Obsuccession

You said, *Come on in, the water's fine.*
So I busted cannonballs off across the ocean and back
and you said, *That's not what I meant.*

I know I took things too far sometimes
but I didn't mean to pass you by.

Every day I would try catching up to you.
Every day you would pull me over
and ask where I was going in such a hurry.

By the time I realized I had missed your point
I took to asking if you would meet me way off
the mark. I'd make you dizzy and hope it felt good.

You're gone now and I get it.
I have to know with my lungs what I missed.
Did you see where the wind went

when it got knocked out of me?
Do you know it was by your side?

# THE MATH

There are nine red lights on the radio towers at the end of my city.
I can see them from the start of my street. I don't know how they
work and have only a vague idea what they do but they've been
playing that lazy blinking game with me since I was a child, sitting in
the backseat of an adult road trip to pick up and drop off stepchildren.
Here's the thing I wondered: *How come my parents didn't love each other
when all they wanted was to love each other?*

It doesn't add up.

I am so much older now, still holding the math in my body like
martial law until it agrees to make sense. The subject of solving
calculated misfortune does not recognize my curfew no matter
how many purple circles I push into my face trying to make whole
numbers of the fractions they framed me in. I have been envious
of easy formulas ever since the day I met you, when this anger got
graphed in spheres and the Pythagoras stormed out of my voice.

I have no idea what he was saying.

I did not retain the kind of information necessary to stand in your
presence and figure remainders. I retained the way I felt that time
I held my breath for twenty-three years. The laws of chemistry
and mechanical engineering escaped in the exhale. I do not yet
know how to take apart an engine block or invest in a money
system so I can buy an airplane and fly away on seventy-five
thousand pounds of baggage.

This is my long division.

There were heartbroken cowboys and abandoned women who I
mistook for whole numbers on the inside of our stereo. My parents
filled the car with them, tricked me into loving heartache as if lonely
was a thing to strive for. My AM and my FM were nearly beaten to
death the day you left.

Subtract this.

When the antenna broke from my parents' car I listened to mile markers cut past the window and thought of good hiding places in our house in case killers came looking for a fat kid. I would have been loads of fun to stab. Porky, and fun to stab. I took out the racks in the oven and hid there because you didn't think I would. It requires empathy and practice, like calculus.

Three hundred and sixty degrees.

It got hot in there so they kept the car window cracked to smoke cigarettes and numb the nighttime while the nighttime shoveled air across the back seat over me like dirty holy moments blown down with the smell of         *I'm quitting.*       *I'm quitting.*       *I quit.*

It is only necessary to wear a seat belt if you're sitting up.

When a ten-year-old boy lays down across the bottom half of a leather right angle traveling 55 mph toward the axis of his parents' choices no one bothers him with what will happen when they swerve across the parallel lines. Thank goodness I dream too fast to get killed in a grown-up car crash.

There is a physics to how we fool ourselves.

It is burning steel rods in my envy when your childhood gets too close to mine.

Here's where I lost your number.

You rode in nice cars with the top down on your way to speak-three-language lessons. They gave you skills you could show off like how to pole vault and when to let go. I wanted you to show me computers and x-ray machines and hand-eye coordination so I could learn to stop my head before it ran off the road.

Teach me equals.

Tutor me to not flinch when I throw both halves of my heart in your face. Let me out of these blinking lights. Get me out of this whiny car full of cowboys and her sadness and the smoke, driving sideways airing out this dirty anger. Kill a fat kid and his need to be heard. Let the martyrs cancel each other out. Hold me open in a window on the beaches. Hold me steady to the wealth and on the charm. No more problems multiplying. Take my remainders.

I've been hiding

in a dark green Cordoba on the highway, back to before your greater-than signs could swallow me. There's not a time I look at a photograph when some part of my body isn't staring in awe of how someone like you was able to figure out the math it took to take our picture. Thanks to the author of the camera I have memorized your image when it's still. I wish you could see what you look like

when you're still here.

# TAUGHT

in the third grade Coach Hendrix dumped
        a parachute onto the gymnasium floor
            and had us spread it out flat
like a bed sheet for windmills

        the whole class stood curious
all the way around the edge of it
knelt down when he told us to
        and gripped with both hands tight

        taut

not letting go
        on the count of three
          we flung our arms above our heads
and ran into the middle

        we ran into the middle
we collided in the middle
we screamed instead of stopping
        today it's not kickball and win

        team

today it is air unfolding
        from the caustic way we loved
        taught to speak in bruises
replaced the words for warmth

        an honest attempt to speak our form
when the safety comes to greet us
we will know it did not come easy
        go easy on this

        explain nothing

hold still from retelling the tragedy
        resistance quits its crashing
        good god resenting safety
has become unnecessary

        dove teeth sunk in a parking lot
festival face in a blanket fort
floodlight lasting fastly
          a carnival held in a cup

        Coach Hendrix

watched me run into the red
        with nearly every blackout
        all the endings gave me blackouts
all the blackouts gave me back

# ATELOPHOBIA

My closest friends have watched me beat this battle brain senseless
for as long as I can remember - banging it against the guardrails,
combing through the loose skin, making a bloody mess, admitting to
every single mistake in an effort to come clean clean cleaner – frenetic
attempts to get it right, stand upright, pseudo-heal a babbling body,
swab a swab around inside another wide open wound. Knife fight in
my ego. Hyper considerate hate wad. I know what cards I showed
you. I know whose tables they're on. I know how often they laid
there alone. It was my choice to offer you that much information. It's
no surprise I want the powers of a boomerang. You shouldn't have
given a grinder food for thought.
Stop.

That was then. It was an unnecessary attempt to acknowledge every
flaw, confess you every ugly, expose these crooked caves, highlight
the fine print. I am a habit for fault lines, derailing the details to
own it. I owned how relentlessly guilty I went with the hope that if
I finally got to be beautiful no one would hold it against me, that I
might deserve arrival instead of trading back for shame.
I didn't want you finding out later, like it matters now.
Stop.

I am not here to disrespect your expectations or steamroll anyone's
gift. I don't want to step on your toes. I apologized: for where I came
from: for looking like that: for spinning out. I spun out on spinning
out. I habitually cultivated every single insecurity by thinking it until
I spoke it until I lived it until it represented me in towns where I
stayed for any longer than a few days. People saw me when I lost the
smile inside their ten thousand nitpick questions. I grew so goddamn
impatient. Misfire.
Stop.

Desperate, greedy, beat-up brickmouth. I repeated myself again. I
retold where I came from with new words. New distractions. Still
believing the story. A river runs rife with guns at the bottom. I tried
endearing myself to you from the bottoms up. Guns blazing. Eyes
blazing. Words blazing. There are still calluses on my throat from the
day you walked out on my voice. I peeled them back to the root of
envy, stared down the barrel of a tragedy habit, pulled the pinched
skin away from the hinge. I came unhinged. The weight of my head
collapsed in on itself like a camping cup. I used martyrs for matches
but love is not a forest fire.
Stop.

# START

I was mad at all the years I lost on being mad.

Unfair is a domino snowball.

I've been lonely for a long time now, hoping anyone I perceive as better than me will scoop me up on a night-kite rescue mission and love me so hard I can finally forget about this feeling left inside from all of the years my blood was boiling.

> *Dear Buddy,*
> *it doesn't work like that.*

*If anyone ever loves you as hard as you've been dreaming, chances are you will not believe them until you accept yourself.*

*Let an easy answer kick us in the pants.*

*If I accept it, this will all be over.*

# FOUNDER'S KEEPER

Escape was a rewind button stunt
water falling
from the ground back up.

Attach me to any self portrait
where the back of my head
is mistook for the front.

# SELF-PORTRAIT

A Norwegian painter named Odd Nerdrum
paints sick and moist things. He got lost in
the down side of dead as if dead was
a horrible place. I saw his whole collection
of work in a too big barbell of a book
gobbly as his name. Odd Nerdrum hurt
like a melted pistol whip, overcooked cream
in the middle, burn victim on a pier, ice pick
bristles and bricks. He painted the worst
hurts of high school on the walls of my jungle
stomach, warm-blooded balloon in my throat,
pulled apart pencil teeth, sawed-off
chatter slut, obesity shit on the beach.
It was a dead horse suicide orgy. Odd
Nerdrum painted self portraits without the proper
postage. I remember the one of him with a boner.
I found it daring because he is not a clean man.

It is not brave to be disgusting or unresolved.
I am not proud of a habit to haunt myself
even when it works in the bookends. I wore
my dancing shoes out in the bookends.
I wore a hole in the heel of a canvas, soiled my sheets
of umbilical paper, self-indulgent self-portrait maker,
an inspired pathetic critic who would not let it
rest. Let it rest. These honeysuckle sickles. Odd Nerdrum.
We cannot continue to turn ourselves in for the mess
we left when we tried coming clean. I will say it
once more and then leave: from 1974 until 2003
(and some days through 2000 and now)
I painted ugly self-portraits on purpose
to trail the trigger ditch back to my mother
to show you the fissure they left in her breath
from when they came in to burn out the leech
from where she planted a man in her words
to protect me. He was a candy ass maggot wax

mustard seed. Odd Nerdrum, we are a constellation
of starting points living in the image of a finish line
but it is not our place to try and keep pace with
all of these things that we wish to feel least.
It is to build us an easier easel day for dissolving
a difficult dream. It is playing a grand typewriter time
until they call us by our names, we runners of the risk
of purpose, my blueberry eye in the smoke, you hammer
the size of a watertrain threaded through the barrel
of a telescope. Even if they smash our birthmarks off
they will call us by our names. I, some fancy finger work
and you, all the scholarly words you're worth, Odd Nerdrum,
we have finally here been accounted for and it is written
on our empty graves that *After everything still I stayed*
and I mean it.

I stayed. I stayed. I stayed.

If there's anything I've come to understand it's that I left
my body to tell you these things and did not lock the door
behind me. I have told you my story in stencils, a cut out
image of bread. It was a rigid appointment with faith
in a barbell of a book. My name is Buddy Wakefield
and though I have many self-portraits, this is the one
of me with a boner. I find it daring because I am not
a clean man.

# SANBORN, NY

Behind the garage was a stack of cement slabs.
There were skyscraper green construction paper leaves
taped to the top of four round ice cream buckets
stacked up to look like a palm tree. There were two

palm trees. They were props from a play
in Cub Scouts. Mom helped me load them into the back
seat of a dark green Cordoba instead of throwing them
away. When we got home

I carried two palm trees out behind the garage,
renamed them Ninjas of the Great Green Hair,
then beat the shit out of them for sneaking up on me.

We had a flag pole and a gravel driveway. Mom did yard work
and I did room to wander. I used a turquoise aluminum bat
with a black rubber handle. I batted gravel to the cornfield.
I batted a softball through two garage window panes
for the same reason I'll stick a spoon through crème brûlée.

There was a tree in the corner of the cornfield where I told myself
secrets I did not keep. I have not taken time to hold any tighter.
Such a monster was made of those days I nearly forgot
about the grapevine and clothesline. The brand new yellow
aluminum siding.

Thank you for the room with five windows and the foam
mattresses so I could wrestle the whole neighborhood
and for the dining room chairs so I could wrestle
the whole neighborhood from the top turnbuckle.

Mom, were you pinned under cookie dough
and blood back there? Did you know that
when the snow came I used a stack of cement slabs
to climb to the roof of the garage?

Did you know I would have invited you up
and pointed out a tree with my bat
where you could go to get ready
for the violence we caused ourselves?

# It Happened

the glass was cleaned for them

they walked easily

spread out like privacy

smooth center of a schoolyard children

moved upward safe in bird slopes

in warm spots

on a break in the clouds

a picture of a picture

smiling smart families holding on

thick sweaters and schoolbooks

backpacks filled with porch swings

a future courtyard's wide

fountain in a marble ballroom

bundled in the music hall

comfortable starfish story

circling ripples outward

reassurance in the air

they all felt sharp and crisp

bread baskets

spilling talent spiders out of their eyes

crawling into me

rich like the mothers

who had enough arms to raise them

# MONKEY ENOUGH

there was a family I dreamed of making and of loving

driving back roads New York upstate

smelt food-smoke wood-smoke good-smoke

rose up smoke from the chimney

freshly baked cedar quilt

flannel cake

cobblestone tire swing coveralls

haystack tractor porchcan dance

I was a functional country song in my head some day

I saw socks rub their feet together on our coffee table

and watched myself watching the finals

you cooked me breakfast

my children thought I had big hands

I was not afraid to BBQ for men who understand ballistics

# HURLING CROWBIRDS AT MOCKINGBARS

If we were created in God's image
then when God was a child
he smushed fire ants with his fingertips
and avoided tough questions.

There are ways around being the go-to person.
Even for ourselves.
Even when the answer is clear
like the holy water gentiles were drinking
when they realized

"Forgiveness is the release of all hope for a better past."

I thought those were chime shells in your pocket
so I chucked a quarter at it
hoping to hear some part of you respond on a high note.

You acted like I was hurling crowbirds at mockingbars
then you abandoned me for not making sense.
Evidently I don't experience things as rationally as you do.

For example, I know mercy
when I have enough money to change the jukebox
at a gay bar.

You know mercy whenever
someone shoves a stick of morphine
straight up into your heart.

Goddamn it felt amazing
the days you were happy to see me.

So I smashed a beehive against the ocean
to try and make our splash last longer.
Remember all the honey
had me looking like a jellyfish ape
but you walked off the water
in a porcupine of light, strands of gold
drizzled out to the tips of your wasps.

This is an apology letter to the both of us
for how long it took me to let things go.

It was not my intention to make such a production
of the emptiness between us,
playing tuba on the tombstone of a soprano
to try and keep some dead singer's perspective alive.

It's just that I could have swore you sung me a love song back there
and that you meant it
but I guess some people just chew with their mouth open.

So I ate ear plugs alive with my throat, hoping they'd get lodged
deep enough inside the empty spots that I wouldn't have to hear you
leaving, so I wouldn't have to listen to my heart keep saying
all my eggs were in a basket of red flags, all my eyes to a bucket
of blindfolds in the cupboard with the muzzles and the gauze.

I didn't mean to speed so far out and off, trying to drive
your nickels to a well
when you were happy to let those wishes drop.

But I still show up for gentleman practice
in the company of lead dancers
hoping their grace will get stuck in my shoes.
Is that a handsome shadow on my breath, sweet woman,
or is it a cattle call in a school of fish? Still

dance with me. Less like a waltz for panic,
more for the way we'd hoped to swing
the night we took off everything
and we were swinging for the fences.

Don't hold it against my love. You know I wanna breathe deeper
than this. I didn't mean to look so serious, didn't mean
to act like a filthy floor, didn't mean to turn us both
into some cutting board
but there were knives stuck
in the words where I came from.
Too much time in the back of my words.
I pulled knives from my back and my words.
I cut trombones from the moment you slipped away.

And I know it left me lookin' like a knife fight, lady.
Boy I know it left me feelin' like a shotgun shell.
You know I know I might've gone and lost my breath
but I wanna show you how I found my breath to death.
It was buried under all the wind instruments
hidden in your castanets. Goddamn. If you ever wanna know
how it felt when you left, if you ever wanna come inside
just knock on the spot
where I finally pressed *stop*

playing musical chairs with your exit signs.

I'm gonna cause you a miracle

when you see the way I kept God's image alive.

"Forgiveness is for anyone
who needs safe passage through my mind."

If I really was created in God's image
then when God was a boy
he wanted to grow up to be a man.
A good man.

And when God was a man - a good man - he started
telling the truth in order to get honest responses.
He'd say,

*Yeah, I know... I really should've worn my cross.*
*Again. But I don't wanna scare the gentiles off.*

*That is not what I came here to do.*
He said,

*I'm pretty sure*
*I just came here to love you.*

*Reverend Kathianne Lewis spoke the lines "Forgiveness is the release of all hope for a better past," and "Forgiveness is for anyone who needs safe passage through my mind." She was quoting someone else when she spoke them. I cannot confidently state the writer responsible for those two lines. Sources often point to Lily Tomlin as well as Anne Lamott. Of any piece I perform, the first of those two lines is most complimented. I lay no claim to those quotes, only thanks for them.*

# FOR CARLEY AUCTEL'S ADMIRER

*- Here I sit, brokenhearted swastika*
*- fuck you fuck off fuck this*
*- fags burn in hell*
*- Jesus was a truck driver [shit smear]*
*- died for our sins on the cross*
*- bore the burden is risen in the utmost*
*- to the highest is my savior oh Lord*
*- obama bin laden suck bush [dry cum drip]*
*- need dick call harold call now for pussy*
*- don't drop your toothpicks in the toilet or the crabs will pole vault*

To bathroom stalls and dressing rooms across America,

You have not yet revealed your full potential for progress in the same way television has failed to release good news, and schools have failed to teach children from the get-go that everything is connected.

(Though I am impressed by your penchant for accurately-drawn cocks of various proportions. In fact, the cock-to-vagina ratio sketched on rest-and-dressing-room walls globally is staggering to say the least. Vaginas are too complex, I suppose.)

But on July 11, 2007, there was discovered a dinosaur language written as clear as the air itself, flawless like a tear duct, someone astonishing among the graffiti swamp and fecal particulate had written on the men's room wall at the Grog Shop in Cleveland, Ohio with red marker inside a dirty white gangland tag the following words:

*Carley Auctel*
*you are beautiful*
*and you rock my socks*
*and you are perfect.*

# IN LANDSCAPE

there is a chance you will show up          laughing
made of fortified fan blades and ferris wheel lights
true of heart and best foot forward
our long-awaited love          made easy

remember for sure          no doubt          these things

the joy          we are a point of complete
this life          standing guard over your solitude
my eyes          are monsters for most things approaching
                    I'm probably gonna need a hand with that
this heart
this sleeve          neither one of them things is all that clean

but the rain          my lucky number
been doin' her part to make things right
for the light bulbs and the bruises

hiding holy water
was not my *forte* this life

          *forte*
          is French
          for blanket fort

I have trusted my corners to revolving doors
but am fluent in getting better          we are
fluent in bouncing back          lifting quickly          learning fast

our courage is a natural habitat

we're gonna build a body to keep          the wolves out
hold my house          you humble barbarian          this door only opens
for the remarkable now          so we will both show up

remarkable

114

speak your peace from the *I can do anything*
say it clearly          follow through

on runways
in turbulence
there is a book living inside your chest
with dilated instructions on how to make a safe landing
it was written                    for crash landers

                          thank you

I am coming home to listen

              please forgive me my distractions

there's a freckle on your lip          it's a national
archive              give it to my ear
so you can see what I mean          here

hold my breath

I will be                              right                        back

there are gifts hidden beneath these lungs
slide your hand over my mouth
and I will speak them in hilltop      in hang glider
from the loyalty of a landscape      silk in a sand-
paper offering plate          the jacket
on a handsome man          that lip          Sweet Grape          you
cannibal                    kiss my eyes with it until they see
          what it is that I wish to write down

your name          film strips of prayer          ribbons
of a garden in stereo          driftwood welded
to the guest house          ring finger wrapped
in a horseshoe nail          I will meet you by
the eighth daydream in the wide open purpose
of a locomotive coming to a stand still with the sea

like thumb on pulse       you watch what happens
when the air erupts into suction cups
opening up to breathe
like the love in my lungs took the tip of my tongue
and finally taught it how to read    you five-acre ladder-
backed pearl book pouring from a pileated
chest of earth    I know                          our story
may look like octopus ink to the rest
of the breath in this world still flying in
under the radar              holding to a pattern of worth

come closer      you guests of honor
chickens        stay off the porch

we are the house gift-wrapped in welcome mats
your dinner's on the table in thanks of that
and the loaves of chocolate toast    the book of Job
and of jet propulsion      raincoats floating
                                  in a rocket ship

we were playing naked checkers in bed

it is an utterly epic arrival
every time I get to see you again

god       this is what I've been
                  talking about
for like thirty-seven years

a true story        of ocean throat        of grace        the holy
goodness glory I was praying to your face            my man
this is what I meant and this is what I'm meant
to do            so sit me down            inside us now
and let me praise the greatest      good in you

by laying down my weapons
including the shield
in rest    inception          for real

116

on cue          my friend          you came                    your name
well lit                     stenciled on the walls of Fremont County
years before we ever met
in landscape     in scope          and so
wing tipped
                    I wrote it
          down
                              to the ground
          you  walk on
with the heels      of my helium shoes

*put your ear to the sky*
*and listen*
*my darling*

*everything whispers*
          *I love you*

*\*The Junkyard Ghost Revival (Andrea Gibson, Derrick Brown, Anis Mojgani and I) found the line "Put your ear to the sky and listen my darling everything whispers I love you" stenciled on a wall in Fremont County (Shoshoni, Wyoming; population: 649). I typed the line into a search engine and discovered that it comes directly from a song called "Christmas" by Jason Anderson. When I asked Jason for permission to use it, the kind New Englander was very surprised to learn how far his voice had carried.*

117

# FLOATING DEVICE

## 1

Last night I dreamt I was on an airplane full of babies wearing very expensive diapers and texting newspapers back and forth to each other, or playing Sudoku in the full and upright position. All of them were growing disjointed and passive aggressive, pissed off with me because I wouldn't stop crying like a stabbed cow stuck in a foghorn. Fuck pretzels. One of the chubbier, huffier babies finally plucked the pacifier out of his mouth, heaved up a breath from under the silk bib across his tailored vest, looked directly at me and said, *Dude... seriously?*

## 2

I kick the backs of seats when I don't get the life I think I need. Do not block the aisles if I experience absolution. There should be enough room to dance in it. A room the size of all the wisdom I have so far gathered up but have not yet consistently handled well. When I tell you I need to be alone what I mean is that I don't want you to see me changing the batteries on my confidence or the mercury levels in my floundering. Bring me back my father. Let us speak of living.

## 3

My father was a police officer. I wanted to follow in his footsteps so I could legally kick in doors, mutherfucker put your hands on my head and hold me by the greener grass I'm growing. Rip out patches from the back and show me what it is I forget to be thankful for.

## 4

Officer Beasley showed up to my dream with a handful of French burnt peanuts. Those were my favorite when I was a kid. He wouldn't know. He held a need to be forgiven on his shoulder. I saw it in his heart. His heart was in my dream. My father's heart was in my dream. It was absolutely beating. He wore it like a badge and I forgave him. Absolutely.

I showed him the bedroom of the man I loved. I showed a need for him to be proud of me. My father is proud of me. The man I loved was not in the room. There was a door on the other side. It was not an emergency exit so I walked through it

5

by myself.

# IRIS

If bright pink and bright orange settled into one color,
with yellow heightened, diminished or popped
in the black, that's what I see when I close my eyes.
Iris, get in here.
Tell me how much the light got through.
Relax your language, just say what you see.

*I saw a hand held up*
*like a cup*
*rooted at the wrist*
*like a tree*
*built from staircases*
*I climbed to the tip*
*of the ring finger*
*and made myself*
*a promise*
*to cross the finish line*
*as is*
*no matter what*
*this too.*

When I say my ABC's there is a series of descending
movements, deeply sideways from A to Z.
The way from L to P writes just like a waterslide, Iris,
you caught me halfway home. I already know what color
my house is on the outside.

# March 14, 2006

On my bedroom wall there is artwork
of a baboon sitting on a stool

like a life model
looking sincere and tired.

Printed underneath him is the word
SURVIVORS.

Today I image-searched the word
LIVERS.

I printed the clearest picture of a liver
and hung it next to the baboon.

> Home,
> Seattle.

# WHEN A GUN BEGINS TO BE GUN

Once I stayed after church to join a prayer circle
because I was concerned about the way I unlove people.

The circle was all women with soft voices, holding
hands, eyes closed. Each woman would pray

thanks then pass to the next person with a slight squeeze
to her left. When she squeezed my right hand I began

to speak. My deep voice accidentally crushed out and tackled
the soft space. I felt the room stop. Only one thought

spread through me in the pause
before I continued praying out loud with them

*Do not let every man who came before you*
*speak for you now.*

# Sick White Beast

I choose to politely ask myself
to step aside
if I am in my own way.

If I do not get out of my own way
I choose to call a friend
who will have me removed.

# WATER GUN

You approached me like a molehill
in the hour of my mountain.
There was a shovel tucked
into the small of your crooked back
where the water guns used to go
and I didn't see you reach for it, Squirt.

When I welcomed you in
trust came first.
There was no need for a cavity search.
You took advantage of this and hid
an entire sandcastle deconstruction kit
right behind that big, bright eye, tried
tunneling through me like an ulcer
in my child side.

I don't go looking for snake bites on breathing tubes
but there you were, teeth sunk in, caught red
no-handed and rattled. Ya got rattled
when I caught ya, became irrational
when I caught ya like a balloon we filled up
and let loose.

It was easy for you to take the wind out of my sails.
All you had to do was suck.
You're so clever
the way you slit the big out of people
then pat them on the fault lines.
Remember when I would scratch your back
then you would hold up my weakness and stab it
with the backscratcher? Felt like

a child again, the way we both let me hate
myself as hard as I possibly could. I still look
just like you in the mirror some days,

still talk like you when the time's right
with that flashy dance floor tongue
and your slicked back mirror ball face
reflecting all the ways you would destroy yourself
if there was no one else around.

You finally wore out the welcome mat, wiped
your feet off across my door like that, arms spread out
like an abacus, telling me I could count on you.
I ended up with zero, watching those loose lips slide
sunk ships back and forth across your expiration date.

You built a corner around me because I couldn't be
backed into one, stared down the barrel of a cheap shot
and pointed it straight at my smile. Gunning down easy
targets is for beginners, Billy Kid. There is no high noon
in my heart today. You will not shoot holes
in the dam. People drink here.

Stand there and call it my life if you want to. Trigger
every inch of my spine. This spine will not quit
my blood when it's boiling. My blood was not built
to rest. You can leave that up to my breath. This breath
is the fairest way. It is the only instrument left on the stage
that I came to this world already knowing
how to string and tune up, strum and reload,
whistle and fiddle, harpoon it and play.

If living really is the greatest revenge
then I want you to know my breath.

And if we really do
get what we give
then I give up
so I can get up.

# THE SIZE AND SHAPE OF ALL THINGS ROLLING

By the time my fingernails had split
and cut their way back in
toward the knuckle grit

I had already chewed these teeth
clear down to the dirty nubs
from chattering about how hard I hit bottom again

how far I had to climb up out of it
shovel myself off and start over
been doing that long as I can remember

as if it were my calling
as if my name were Helter Skelly
rising from falls I keep taking in vain

just for a reason to stand here,
looking like another loose jawbone
hinged on a tilt-a-whirl.

The question was,

*If god can do anything,*
*can he can make a rock so big*
*that even he can't lift it?*

The answer is

*Yes, all he has to do*
*is commit*
*to defeating himself.*

# A HOLE IN GOD

you appeared like a body bag
            fulla hymnal books
unzipped in half I

            never saw so many door jams fall
outta anyone's mouth
            into math like that when

Tennessee put its crooked smile
            on a wadded up map
and sent you packin'

West

            good

gospel gospel got god
stuck to the rock he made and
            he mighta made it larger than us
            or it mighta served to save this place
sure I coulda swore I heard you calling
for a shot at a grip on vice
            doesn't mean your mouth was moving
            doesn't mean I even heard you right

all I know is that your skin keeps calling
and I don't care if it's a busted flint
            'cause every time you pull your thumb down on it
            I get [up up] back up to my feet

            again

all of them

move move
like an offering plate
on'm one by one

it's a penchant for a savior
a tendency to *overrun*
whatever shook do not get shook up
whatever's lost you don't get lost
even if they say you must give more than
everything you ever offered up

I know a voice does not come easy
I know the words fell out in bites
I know the moment when
the abandonment
looked a lot like flight
you pulled whatever got left

inside

out right

# JEAN HEATH

In the end, Jean Heath's home was filled
with people who claimed to know her better than
they actually did. They swapped tissues and embellished
stories to appear closer to Jean Heath than they actually were
in the same way wearing expensive clothes on Sunday apparently
brings wealthy Baptists closer to god than they actually are.

It was mostly unfamiliar faces who seemed to be looking
for due credit on the role they may or may not have played
in the life of Jean Heath, networking their sorrow and searching
like they always do in every death for the gate to restoration
as if this life really wants us to stay here.

They took turns crying on Jean Heath's face as a sign
she would be missed. There was so much crying that I, the care-
giver, could hear Jean Heath's bed sheets slap together when
she moved. And there was food. Holy hams and jam, y'all, there was
so much food. At least an acre of it. Across the kitchen countertops
and over the tables, falling out of the refrigerator and along the arms
of chairs. There were plastic cups with names written on them.
Sometimes twice. Sometimes two cups. Kids lose shit.

There was ambrosia with snot on it, cornbread with tears in it,
black-eyed peas with the trembling ladle, strawberry rhubarbed
wire pie, melty vanilla ice creamed pulp, and there were perfect
middle squares still left in the brownie pan. I know who ate the end
pieces. The little ones were warned, death is a very serious matter so
they had better not act up or else they would be forced to pick their
own switch and get whipped with it.

We were tricked into fearing the ways we will leave this planet.

Emily Beezhold was 26-years-old that day when she came to play
piano for her best friend Jean Heath, age 87, who lay flat and velvet
on her death-bed, lookin' like the front pew of a gospel church
without the guilt.

When the other guests asked Emily how she knew Jean Heath Emily thought of Jean's lonely days on the porch when no one came to visit, when the money ran out, when the yearning for love haunted her, taught her how heavy the hollows are, how crippled a memory can make ya, how sometimes she'd cry so hard her throat locked out all the noise.

*I trust you people about as far as I can throw you,*
Emily said,
*and I can't throw you.*

The candles inside her piano keys are why Emily's fingertips burn when she plays. It's why she plays like that. It doesn't scare Jean Heath when she plays like that. She bangs both feet down on the sustain pedal, bouncing, and she sings like that; teeth all gripped out like a hallway howling

*Holler holler,* she sang, *I'm goin' home.*
*Might be a little bit bit but*
*I'm gonna show'em.*
*Might be dirty,*
*might be skinny like water*
*but there's a hole in god*
*and I'm not gonna fall down in there.*

And that day when she played, sometimes with her knuckles, mostly with her memory, she remembered a true story she read once, in a book about self-acceptance, where a daughter sits next to her mother who's in a coma until one morning before dawn when the mother wakes up, looks very clearly and very intently at her daughter and says, *Ya know, my whole life I thought there was something wrong with me.* Then the mother shook her head as if to say, *what a waste,* before drifting back into her coma and dying several hours later.

You knew she would. These stories we give each other are just different reasons for begging you to stay, but nobody's gonna stay here. Emily knows Jean Heath won't stay. She's cool with that. They both just wish they would have known a little sooner about this life that every loss doesn't have to cost so much, doesn't have to hit so heavy, doesn't have to get so dirty.

*Dirty dirty like Christ*
*on his little brown mule.*
*I was baptized in tap water*
*and I never really went to school.*
*I got a hunger for you,*
*I got a hunger for you,*
*but I never,*
*but I never,*
*but I never really came through.*

Jean Heath was tender and bossy when she finally called Emily
Beezhold to her bedside. While she was happy that her house
smelled like a baked good, and she was thankful
for the best of the gestures from the guests in the bedrooms,
and she was wondering about some of the recipes,
Jean Heath was very clear and very intent in the moment she finally
pulled Emily Beezhold's ear down to her mouth and said inside of it,

*Get these people out of my house.*
*I've never died before.*
*And I'm gonna enjoy it.*

★*The two choruses sung by Emily Beezhold in* Jean Heath *were written*
*by Timmy Straw. The previous poem,* A Hole In God, *is inspired by and*
*warmly dedicated to Tim.*

131

# Open Letter To The People Of The Future

Before the earth finally opened up and swallowed its own surface to make room for you, The People of the Future, there was still enough time to write this down:

By now you have found my gym bones jammed between the door frame, crushed under my school desk, the gum still stuck in my hair. Yes, it was a dumb place to try and hide from the end of the world, but I am young and passionate enough to believe that my heroes are giving us good directions.

There is no way for me to know how many of our street signs and libraries you have already studied, or if you can even tell the fact from the fiction scrawled between the lines in our outdated text, before finding me here, buckled like a one-way accordion, but I will do my best to fill in the blanks in chronological chaos.

Here goes:

We came from monkeys and tadpoles, rainwater and clay, accidents and gods held together in the hallelujahs, pulled apart like a spider web. We were dripped down and stretched thin. Everything was humid and stuck together. I was a slide whistle in a finger trap. There are tricks to getting out without making sound.

Here's the truth:

All the vampires you read about in our books before getting to me as a detail, those were fiction. But the inspiration we got from our vampire songs, that was real. I saw it with my very own eyes. There is a point you should no longer watch. I've got a hands down case against passion; desperate burning bloodsucker.

Listen carefully:

When we found the West Coast we felt like paradise had to be more, more than what it already was, when what it already was was more than enough, but we couldn't fit enough in our mouths, so most of us took to barking around in our wild distended voices, bought animals we couldn't take care of, taught them to depend on us, then left them alone.

In the future, don't do that. There were puppies deserted in crates for decades of hours of howling, dying inside for a bone while their owners were fetching for good intentions.

If you're gonna make a point don't miss it. Even our finest forgot how to help a small thing from hurting. Even good hearts know how to turn bad touch and genocide into clichés just to make room for more comfort.

More comfort. More comfort. My goodness. My word.

Sometimes all you will notice in my letter is a tail wagging when you walk in the door. If you're reading this, go home. I will tell you what happened, but you have to go home:

It was a black hole that finally ate us. We went looking for it so it ate us. There. Now you know. We were swallowed by the tremendous cavity jammed between forgiveness and people.

I was learning how to fill in the gap when you came, inserting myself into space, converting my mind into wine. I was cake decorating the emptiness. We were all rewriting the sky, with fireworks and satellites, heisting the image of stars, our refineries pumping out cloud cover stink to bury the mountain of timeshares we sold to The People of the Future.

*And I:*

I was clearly very *very* important, until I wasn't. When I say *I,* I usually mean *we.*

*We:*

Pushed cigarettes into our face, then with the other hand danced around the edge of this place to feel worthy of making a statement or to keep from feeling alone, and that worked, until it didn't. Yesterday, we worried that when you, The People of the Future, find us here, it will be because you are digging for something more, something more than you already are, as if anything could ever be more. Stop creating.

Go home.

Put me and my letter and this ridiculous desk back into the ground with the prescriptions and the computers and Henry Darger's alarming heart.

Stop dying. Stay still. We have turned into poems on paper. There are things we did well. Wad me up.

For you, there is still so much time left to cease convincing each other that it is too late to rest assured. Give that honest head of yours a snowball's chance to climb back down through your throat and into your body so it can see just how good you look when you're not compared to anything.

*You and me:*

We look good in these shoes and a swagger talk. We learned to walk well in these words is all, even when they're hard to read, dirty and dug from the ground. At least they speak directly to us, because our weather is perfect, and our timing is perfect, and because I know that you, The People of the Future, will dig here.

Even the Earth
when she ate us
had her soft spots.

# HORSEHEAD

When I rode off into the sunset
there was no blackout
or camera behind me.
I did not recede into the distance.
I was still very much present
with what I had left behind.
My horse was thirsty
from how far I ran him
and your god as my witness
I ran him
until I rode into town here and realized
I'm not the end of a movie.

I am done playing sunsets for lonely.
My best days are the days I see clearly.
So I had hoped
to come clean here perfectly
for you and the whole saloon
but there is no polish on the table tonight.
Expect rough spots then
when I show you my cards.
These hands we were dealt
may splinter.
The spades could get under your skin.
I was living with them under my skin.
They were digging up into my film strip.
I was riding with them stuck in my heart.

It is work to ride head up and holy here.
It is painters with slack in their brush.
Painters all jacked up
on stampede dust
just trying to get it right.
I've been trying to get it right.
I've been learning here how to grow larger
than the monsters alive in my dreams
swinging a crow bar
out of my whistle
grand pianos out of my rust.

I shot typewriter keys out of cannons I keep
aimed at the bandits alive in my trust.

There were bandits alive in my trust
come to burn down the verbs
left alone in my blood
barkin' like dogs in a combine
my horsehead sweat
like a war on a land mine
jawbone chomp at the bit
like a bear trap telegraph
I know I look
like a bleeding dot
by now from where you stand
where there is mad dash
and such wild west
and it is raining down locomotives
on a horse who might not have a name
but who carries a trough in his chest
empty as it may be today
from feeding bandits disguised as the Pony Express
comin' up spades and splinters
my workhorse spittin' out hammers and ink.

There is a colony of bad fathers
who built this place
still alive in the way I was led to think
like a snake
who can shed its own crucifixion
or a midnight rider who leads his beast
under whip of the daylight sky.
That's why I looked like gallop cursive
when you held me under
the horizon line
to magnify
every single silver screen I stole
riding high on my filthy electric whale
like a bullet through a junkyard ghost.

Ya know, I don't care to be good, Sheriff.

I care to be whole.

So read what it says in my buckles boy.
*Take your sunset out of my rise.*
I will not send you sailing if you came here to drive
and I know you came here to drive.
That's why it reads *don't give up* on your saddle
like I wrote *won't give up* on my life
like I've been typing my name
on a horse I drove
through the desert as sure as a river he ran
and I swear on my shadow he wouldn't turn back
no matter how much slack I typed into his neck.

Not everyone wants to go home
to get the sunset painted back into their bones
to have the law with all that slack in its love
pretending to save me.
You don't need to save me.
I already did that myself
when your god as my witness
never turned up.

There was a typewriter
buried alive in that horse

the one I rode to get out of the flood.

# BRAWL

Today I got into
a bar fight
in my head
that I could not
possibly win.
But I did.

I did win.

# Bio

Buddy Wakefield aims to cause a disarming de-haunting of accidents.
He is pursuing a career in judgment suspension but sometimes wants
to blend in so badly he forgets his purpose and worries that everyone
else is doing it right, or wrong. He once sat on top of the whole
world and told it jokes about the ocean until everybody crumbled
into tattoos of bakeries. It smelled good. Felt right. We laughed.
So much. Sometimes, he studies propellers because they can make
themselves invisible. Buddy has collected enough humongous
titles to be crushed under their weight. There are no stunt doubles
performing the accidents in his work or the bursts of beast in his
behavior. There is a recurring theme in his nightmares where he
wakes up only to realize that whatever supposedly awful thing was
stalking him was really just trying to help. His interests include
cephalopods, chopping wood and untrembling, unless trembling is
imperative to a successful dance move.

# JOB DESCRIPTION

Show your work.

# WREST

April 17, 2006

"The winner of the rat race
is a rat." – ?

Before the first full day of meditation started, there was a day of
checking in and getting situated and Formica countertops and thin
crust carpet and durable white plastic patio chairs inside. Shoes came
off at the door.

I like being on time.
I'm good for it.
Showed up at the beginning.
I went for a long walk in the field while folks trickled in
and registered.

There was a black and white cat who greeted me in the field as if to
say, *"You're on the right path. Now you must pet me until I can take petting
no longer."* So I pet him. A lot.

That night during the greeting session we were asked not to pet the
cats. They come from neighboring properties. We were to practice
noble silence and maintain equanimity without distraction.

Throughout the ten days I steered clear of the little guy.
I did not give him a name. It was a cat.
Staley, probably.

I watched a woman succumb to the pressure of the purr and pet him
somewhere between days six and nine. She petted him real good for
two quick strokes then refocused. I wanted to run across the path and
the yard, arms up and arched, fingers curly, screaming, *"Pet the kitty!"*

I observed my sensations instead.

There was another cat with no interest in people. She sported
borderline mange and walked with the urgency of Snuffalufagus on
tranquilizers. She maintained equanimity and had no desire to be
cuddled.

She was at least 127 years old in cat years best I could tell. She was also in no mood to have psychic communication with me. There were several black-and-amber caterpillars and a woodpecker who were into it though. We totally connected.

★★★

I believed in Santa Claus until somewhere around the second grade. There was a consequence for not believing in Santa. No gifts. Exposing the Easter Bunny and other lies followed suit. The tooth fairy fooled me for at least three teeth to my recollection.

For my first twenty-three years, I was scared into believing in a god who would eventually quite literally burn forever anyone who did not strictly adhere to his laws as written by man in a book using language that has long since been subtly (if not overtly) mutilated.

There was my stepsister who stole from the offering plate, who lied more than she spoke. There was my aunt who lost both her legs and most of her family to the lies in which she soaked. There was my dad and the reasons he chose to close the garage door and turn the ignition. There was the fraud of my former employer in Gig Harbor and the millions of dollars he stole and the mountains of hope he crushed just by lying.

There were the days I lied about loving this place.

When I was twenty-four I worked with a family who were completely prepared for Y2K (the supposed end of the planet as we knew it due to a timing glitch in the worldwide web).

They had a house in the middle of Nowhere, Eastern Washington and a thoughtful paper packet packed with loads of useful information, and expectations. I was to consider the packet an invitation. I was being invited to stay with them through Armageddon if I wanted. There were documents and "evidence" and I was convinced. I even went so far as to warn my closest friends (one of whom has still not let me live it down; fair enough). I've believed in more twisted individuals and entities and selves than any of us have the wherewithal to recollect tonight; people and notions whose teachings I planted inside of me only to yield mediocrity, if not thorn, if not cactus, if not fly trap, poison bite, tooth grinder. Sawdust pulls up the stink.

My beliefs have cried wolf more times than I care to remember. I do not type this without a rise in temperature or a little embarrassed. Each time I get fooled I have the exact same dialogue with myself. It goes like this,

*Buddy, do not stop trusting people.*
Then back, *I won't.*

If I lose trust in people, what's that say about how I view myself? A pretty grim reflection.

So in the welcome session on the first night when the teacher of this international Vipassana course, S.N. Goenka, stated on paper his expectations of us, including surrendering our entire selves for ten days to the teachings of Vipassana meditation,
my internal dialogue went,

*Watch out, Buddy!*
Then back, *No shit.*

★★★

I know where I stand now, especially when the ground gives way.

★★★

Alex (the man who lived inside a room which was built inside the room where I stayed) has been practicing Vipassana for over eight years. His eyes are big and curious and shy and welcoming. His clothes hang like burlap sacks. It is easy to want to hug him despite what I suspect would be a hesitant return embrace.

Physical contact is not allowed at the meditation center. No exercising or reading or writing or eye contact or talking or stealing or substances or sexy time or killing even a bug.

I was glad to eat veggie lasagna with Alex on the last day. We were both glad. I clearly got a lot out of the 10-day course. I asked if he lived at the center full time and if he considers himself a monk. He let out a reserve of breath to show being tickled. He told me he had a job at a food co-op and a significant other and a home. My eyes filled with water.

"This is it isn't it? I mean, this is the answer."

I wasn't really asking.

I was experiencing it.

I experience it.

It is not a mystery.

★★★

www.dhamma.org

★★★

I had no idea I wasn't supposed to pet the cat.

...and I remember seein'm break and run off by themselves
and I remember they were full force in song
throwing their bodies around like wands
and I remember clearly
they wanted out.

...and I remember when the train came
they all hopped it
though they never claimed to ride that way
but it was midnight
and it was going to Georgia
and it was free.

# Acknowledgements

Thanks like a Dutch New Year celebration to Dennis Gaens of Wintertuin, and Jan-Wieger van den Berg of Besiendershuis, Nijmegen, Netherlands for the time and space to get the ball rolling on this book.

Meditative appreciation goes out in all directions to S.N. Goenka and Eckhart Tolle, for every reason.

And to my wingman, Andrew "Faye" Gibson, for a safe place to land. Thank goodness.

## About The Author

Buddy Wakefield from Los Angeles, CA by way of Boulder, CO by way of Seattle, WA by way of Baytown, TX by way of Sanborn, NY by way of Shreveport, LA is a three-time Poetry Slam world champion by accident. He likes peanut butter, Vipassana, cheering for exhausted runners and is currently studying propellers because they can make themselves invisible. His website is kept current.

www.buddywakefield.com

# IF YOU LIKE BUDDY WAKEFILED, BUDDY WAKEFIELD LIKES...

*Born in the Year of the Butterfly Knife*
Derrick Brown

*Pansy*
Andrea Gibson

as well as works by Mindy Nettifee, Anis Mojgani, Cristin O'Keefe Aptowicz, Jeremy Radin, Megan Falley, Jon Sands and Brendan Constantine.

# WRITE BLOODY BOOKS

*After the Witch Hunt* — Megan Falley

*Aim for the Head: An Anthology of Zombie Poetry* — Rob Sturma, Editor

*Amulet* — Jason Bayani

*Any Psalm You Want* — Khary Jackson

*Birthday Girl with Possum* — Brendan Constantine

*The Bones Below* — Sierra DeMulder

*Born in the Year of the Butterfly Knife* — Derrick C. Brown

*Bring Down the Chandeliers* — Tara Hardy

*Ceremony for the Choking Ghost* — Karen Finneyfrock

*Courage: Daring Poems for Gutsy Girls* — Karen Finneyfrock, Mindy Nettifee & Rachel McKibbens, Editors

*Dear Future Boyfriend* — Cristin O'Keefe Aptowicz

*Dive: The Life and Fight of Reba Tutt* — Hannah Safren

*Drunks and Other Poems of Recovery* — Jack McCarthy

*The Elephant Engine High Dive Revival* anthology

*Everything Is Everything* — Cristin O'Keefe Aptowicz

*The Feather Room* — Anis Mojgani

*Gentleman Practice* — Buddy Wakefield

*Glitter in the Blood: A Guide to Braver Writing* — Mindy Nettifee

*Good Grief* — Stevie Edwards

*The Good Things About America* — Derrick Brown & Kevin Staniec, Editors

*Hot Teen Slut* — Cristin O'Keefe Aptowicz

*I Love Science!* — Shanny Jean Maney

*I Love You Is Back* — Derrick C. Brown

*The Importance of Being Ernest* — Ernest Cline

*In Search of Midnight* — Mike McGee

*The Incredible Sestina Anthology* — Daniel Nester, Editor

*Junkyard Ghost Revival* anthology

*Kissing Oscar Wilde* — Jade Sylvan

*The Last Time as We Are* — Taylor Mali

*Learn Then Burn* — Tim Stafford & Derrick C. Brown, Editors

149

*Learn Then Burn Teacher's Manual* — Tim Stafford & Molly Meacham, Editors

*Live for a Living* — Buddy Wakefield

*Love in a Time of Robot Apocalypse* — David Perez

*The Madness Vase* — Andrea Gibson

*The New Clean* — Jon Sands

*New Shoes on a Dead Horse* — Sierra DeMulder

*No Matter the Wreckage* — Sarah Kay

*Oh, Terrible Youth* — Cristin O'Keefe Aptowicz

*The Oregon Trail Is the Oregon Trail* — Gregory Sherl

*Over the Anvil We Stretch* — Anis Mojgani

*Pole Dancing to Gospel Hymns* — Andrea Gibson

*Racing Hummingbirds* — Jeanann Verlee

*Rise of the Trust Fall* — Mindy Nettifee

*Scandalabra* — Derrick C. Brown

*Slow Dance with Sasquatch* — Jeremy Radin

*The Smell of Good Mud* — Lauren Zuniga

*Songs from Under the River* — Anis Mojgani

*Spiking the Sucker Punch* — Robbie Q. Telfer

*Strange Light* — Derrick C. Brown

*These Are the Breaks* — Idris Goodwin

*Time Bomb Snooze Alarm* — Bucky Sinister

*The Undisputed Greatest Writer of All Time* — Beau Sia

*What Learning Leaves* — Taylor Mali

*What the Night Demands* — Miles Walser

*Working Class Represent* — Cristin O'Keefe Aptowicz

*Write About an Empty Birdcage* — Elaina Ellis

*Yarmulkes & Fitted Caps* — Aaron Levy Samuels

*The Year of No Mistakes* — Cristin O'Keefe Aptowicz

*Yesterday Won't Goodbye* — Brian S. Ellis

CPSIA information can be obtained
at www.ICGtesting.com
Printed in the USA
FSOW01n1144230717
36418FS